M Y    H E A R T

# BELONGS

T O    M O M

# MY HEART
# BELONGS
# TO MOM

A Soldier's Letters to His Mom from the Other Side
## ECHATA

**To order additional copies of this book, contact:**
Xlibris Corporation
1-888-795-4274
www.Xlibris.com
Orders@Xlibris.com
110310

# CONTENTS

# INTRODUCTION

My son joined the Army in 2005. He was 18 years old. He was my youngest child and my only son. When he became a teenager, he wanted to go to Arizona to live with his father. His father and I had joint custody in Missouri in case he ever changed his mind and wanted to come home to me. I only saw him a week in the summer and a few days at Christmas. The divorce decree said I was to have him all summer and every holiday. From previous experience with his father I knew this would never happen. When he went to the Army his father would not even give his sister his address because he didn't want her to give it to me. I went to an Army recruiter but his office was closed. I found a Navy recruiter who found out my son was at Fort Hood.

When my letters started coming back "not at Fort Hood," I wrote to the government. I received a reply within a week and started writing and sending packages to him and his buddies. When I first knew he was in Iraq I would wake myself up praying for him and his buddies.

When he came home, I knew he would be hurting because I knew him. I wrote to his commanding officer saying "I could help him." I didn't understand how soldiers feel about no one knowing any weaknesses. He left me an angry message on my phone and told me not to write him. I stopped writing but kept praying.

When he was sent home because of an injury to his hand, I did not get to see him. When he had his accident his sister called and told me to find a friend to come stay with me. She said her phone was going dead and she would call back. I immediately texted a message to her "Is it about Buddy?" When I got off the phone, I googled his name and found out about his death. I was devastated to say the least. I lay on my bedroom floor and cried and cried. His father had told my younger daughter who told my older daughter "that I was not welcome down there (meaning his memorial service)." I kept crying.

Then his father and everyone in the family wanted to talk to me about honoring Buddy's wishes. I did not understand what they wanted from me. I just cried. My older daughter called my younger daughter who was at her father's house with the rest of the family. My older daughter said "What is wrong with you people—don't you understand he is her son." She said she knew they put her on speaker phone. I am sure she said other things but didn't tell me about it. I just kept crying. After a week of their calling—my land line, my office line, my cell phone, I called and talked with my attorney. I texted a message to his father stating my attorney's name and phone number.

I met with my attorney who had drawn up papers for me to sign agreeing to have my son's body cremated. My attorney told me "how can you not go to the memorial service?" I decided to go with my Cherokee cousin Silver Star, my oldest daughter, and oldest granddaughter.

When we went to the church Silver Star introduced me to the minister and color guard. We sat in the back of the church alone and away from everyone else because of my x-husband's words. When I was watching videos of my son, I thought to myself "I wonder what Buddy's tattoo says?" I heard in my head "My Heart Belongs to Mom." It was not until the next day when we met some of his friends, the words were confirmed. My granddaughter asked one of Buddy's friends "what did Buddy's tattoo say?" He said "don't you know?" I said during the service Buddy told me "My Heart Belongs to Mom." The friend became very excited and said, "Yes, yes that is what it said." I am grateful for that friend confirming what was said to me during the service.

The next day we went to the airport to fly home. This was the first time I was in an airport without having the urge to go up to any one in an Army uniform and show them the picture of my son and ask if they knew him. I began writing stories about Buddy hoping it would help ease the pain inside me and then it was as if he were sitting beside me dictating the stories to me at the age he was at the time they happened. These are his stories not mine. I know he just wanted me to know he is okay. He continues to talk to me especially when I am sad. There is one story I included about the "treasured dollar" and my poem about my sorrow. I have never written poetry or written a journal. Any mother who has lost a child knows how I feel. I hope it helps them the way it has helped me. I am lucky I hear my son. I always knew we had special wiring to talk to angels.

Sincerely,

**E-cha-ta**

## The One Who Many Children Love

I wrote the National Archives, St. Louis, MO to receive any information about my son during his Army service years. I also called many Army offices regarding my son. They were always kind and helpful to me. I thank them from the bottom of my heart.

# MEETING MY SISTER

I first met my sisters when I was a few days old. My dad brought her and my older sister to the hospital to see me. She had to sit in the floor board of dad's car because she wet her pants and dad didn't want her to sit on his leather seats. When she first saw me and my mom she ran to mom smiling and that's how we met. She went to school and told everyone she had a Buddy Bear. It was a few years later, when she began to tease me. Both Lee and momma told her to "stop teasing your brother."

She didn't.

After a few minutes of teasing I would lunge for her hair and pull it out. She would scream for momma and Lee who both would say "stop teasing your brother before you are baldheaded."

# BOUNDARIES

I struggled so hard in school because I had my mom's wiring (wiring to talk to angels). I knew she worried about me and blamed herself. It was many years later she learned "we were Heyoka which means Spiritual Clowns and it was our gift from God." She always seemed to know how I was feeling and what I was thinking. One weekend as I did my usual thing of watching sports, discovery channel or the fishing channel, she brought me a bowl of fruit, cheese, crackers, and carrots. She always seemed to know when I was hungry. So I asked her, "Why do you always bring me bowls of food?" She said "aren't you hungry?" Oh, I am hungry but how did you know I was hungry? She just smiled and kissed me. She loved to kiss me.

I remember when I let her know it was not okay to kiss me especially in public. She was going to kiss me in the checkout lane at a supermarket.

I gave her a look that I knew she would get the message.

She said "I'm sorry you looked so sweet standing there." She never kissed me in public again.

Mom understood boundaries well.

# BIG HOUSE/BAD CHOICES-AGE 2

When we lived in the big house, mom always called it the big house because it was big (mom note—7,000 sq. feet). One day she was doing chores and I was playing with patches and my bubble making lawn mower. She didn't know I could go out the door to the garage, open the car door, push the garage door opener and go out the garage. Patches, my bubble making lawn mower machine and I started to the woods. I loved nature even then. My next older sister still could not open her car door or maybe she liked having someone open it for her. Then it happened I heard her calling my name. She seemed upset. She sure could move fast when she didn't know where I was. She said my dad could run faster. But she moved very, very fast when she saw me. She even had a sprain angle. I think she sprain her ankle chasing me.

I was a good climber even then. I think I was two. When I tried to climb the blocks on the front door she moved fast and caught me. She was like that. She was not mad. She just shook her head. My confirmation "bad choice Buddy"

I could climb the big brass pots by the front door. She caught me then shook her head. I know "bad choice."

One of my biggest feats was climbing out of the bed. She was asleep. It was no fun when she was asleep. So I began sneaking in and sleeping on her chest our hearts touching. I loved that sound and being close to her. She was the best mom ever I was sure.

# BABYSITTING IN THE THE BIG HOUSE

One night she actually went out with friends. She liked being with us more. She was like that. She told another sister who was the designated babysitter when she went to bed to be sure to lock the door and sleep in her bed until she came home.

She forgot.

I made my escape to see the stars and talk to the neighbor's dog. I was sitting on the porch when a neighbor came home late from work. He saw me and woke up the neighbors. My mom's friend knew she was never away from us kids.

She was like that.

The friend worried something had happened to the family and was afraid to bring me home. Not long after that my mom drives into the garage.

Just as the door was going down she saw her friend's night gown and put the door back up.

When the neighbor told her what I did she listened and shook her head. "Bad Choice." She was not mad she just kissed me and put me in bed.

She liked to kiss me. She was like that.

The next morning my sister felt very bad. My mom she never got mad just shook her head—"Bad Choice." She was like that. I loved my mom. Mom rarely went after that she always stayed home with us.

# CANDY STORY

One day when we went to get gas at the filling station. Mom and I went in to pay. I wanted candy. She said, "No." There were three funny looking guys in the filling station. I knew bad words from hearing them from others when they were mad. I was a good listener. I could say those words too and began saying those words I heard. Guess what? She picked me up tucked me under her arm and carried me to the car. She was not mad. The funny looking men seemed amused when she carried me out to the car. My mom was strong. She wasn't mad—just put me in my car seat and drove home. She was like that. I loved her. She was like that.

# MOTHER'S DAY LAWN MOWER

One day after my dad moved out of the big house, mom was going to mow the yard. I was scared she would leave like dad had left. I started crying.

She put me on her back and mowed the yard with the lawn mower she bought herself for Mother's Day.

# GARAGE STORY

One day after my dad moved out mom had to put her car in the garage. The garage people took us home. When her car was fixed she was prepared to walk with us to the garage. My sister beside her and me on her back; we took off. I loved piggy back rides.

My sister to my mom's embarrassment and shame shouted to a neighbor "We don't have a car and we have to walk all the way to the garage." Of course, the neighbor took us to the garage to get our car instead of walking. My mom was mortified with shame.

She was a proud woman and resourceful.

She just shook her head—"bad choice."

I learned from that but not my sister.

I liked to make mom happy.

I was like that.

# I HATE THIS SHITTY BOOK

I struggled with reading but my mom would sit for hours helping me with my homework. My most despised book was The Box Car Kids. We took turns for weeks reading out loud to each other. My mom always knew what to do somehow the precise intervention for my needs. When we finished the book she actually thought I should write a report about the book. I wanted to erase it from my memory.

No, not my mom—she helped me write the book report step by step. Funny, how she always knew what to do. I always wondered who she got her information from. Now I know. The angels-messengers of God told her. She was phenomenal.

But back to the book report—She helped me write the name, the author, and what the story was about. She was following a step by step form from school on How to Make a Book Report except in our terms. The final part of the report was saying what I thought about the book. I knew she didn't like it. I wrote "I hate this shitty book." When my mom saw what I wrote, she said "it wasn't nice to use that word but it was my choice."

Boy did I hate it when she said "you choose" when she knew I knew right from wrong. I went to bed.

I know she snuck into my bedroom and opened my backpack. I knew it made her happy when she saw I had changed my report from shitty to stupid. I couldn't understand what the "big deal was."

As I got older I loved to say words to shock her. She would always say "Buddy, we don't say those words."

I still did. She never got mad or upset—just shake her head.

She always knew I did it for effect. She was smart like that.

# MOVE FROM THE BIG HOUSE

One day we were going to have to move from the "big house." Mom worried if we were happy. She wanted to make it the same in the new house. My mom could move from a half million dollar home to a $500 rental and make it feel the same.

I was confused when we moved—I missed the trees. My mom knowing we were sad let us pick out another dog from the dog pound. She said it was good to give a homeless dog a good home. She said he was our rainy day dog because it was raining the day we found Joey.

Joey was a wonderful dog. We hooked him in the back yard. When he would get loose as he often did he would wait at the back door for us to get up and feed him? Joey seemed to know what me and mom were thinking and feeling.

He loved us. We loved him.

My mom had a difficult time finding a house that would take Joey and Patches (our two dogs). She went to the house that was for rent, and found out she could keep the dogs. She started crying at the door and said she would take it. The family living there asked her if she wanted to see the rest of the house. She looked but she seemed to know it was right for us.

She was smart like that—my mom.

It was a good home to stay for a while. We went for walks in the woods and by the river. Mom seemed to know I loved it outside even then. We would sit on the porch at night, swing, and watch the stars and moon come out.

She gave me a good job when we first moved to the rental home. She said I needed to pound every nail on the porch so we would not trip. I loved to pound. Mom was happy. I was happy.

My mom knew which boxes were my boxes and let me unpack some boxes. I found a funny 6 six sided thing with dots on it (dice). I asked mom if she could find me some more. She smiled and said "I will get right on it, Buddy." I was always happy with mom. She didn't find any more cubes but bought more for me when she went to the store. She was like that my mom. (Mom—there were at least 40 boxes to unpack.)

## THE FOREIGN EXCHANGE BABY-SITTER

The best think about moving was my mom made a new friend, Kitty. Everyone loved my mom. They were going out one night and the Kitty's foreign exchange student who lived with them came to our house to baby sit.

After my mom and Kitty left, my sister and I became very rowdy. We seemed to know the foreign exchange student was new at babysitting. He let us have all the popsicles we wanted. When the popsicles began dripping out our mouth because we were so full; we began licking them off the floor.

The babysitter seemed upset when mom got home and told her what we had done. She shook her head I knew what that meant "bad choice." My sister never figured it out the "bad choice look." She was supposed to be the "gifted one." Kitty later told our mom the foreign exchange student almost went back to Germany because of our behavior. My mom just shook her head "bad choice." My sister never figured it out. Mom never knew how many pop cycles we ate and we didn't tell her.

When she was out with friends and having fun, she didn't seem to know what we were up to. She didn't go out much after that foreign exchange student babysat us. She just stayed home with us; Mom was like that she loved us.

## VISITATION WITH DAD

We began going to dad's house one night a week and every other weekend. There was another person at dad's house. She was not like mom. She was a different person. We missed mom. She didn't understand us like mom did.

When we came home from dad's house my mom said she was getting us ninja turtles stuffed animals. She said it was time we slept in our own beds. She would sing us to sleep. I thought my mom had the most wonderful voice. She only sang to us when we went to sleep. Sometimes, we would listen to music at night to go to sleep. We loved the music; that was one thing my sister and I agreed on was we loved the music.

We found out when we were older it was George Winston. When I hear him even now the music makes me happy and calm. I don't know about my sister later, we never discussed it.

## TRIP TO THE LAKE

One day my mom's friend Kitty and we went to the lake. We asked for McDonald's my mother said "wait until we get to the lake." My sister said "Buddy McDonald's at the lake is better." Mom and her friend were laughing. She and Kitty just looked at each other and smiled. We were glad we made them happy. I liked it when mom was happy. We were not sure why.

## NATIVE AMERICAN HERITAGE/SPIRITUALITY

One day my mom brought home sacred animal cards and a book about the cards. She said she wanted to teach us about our heritage. We did not know what she meant by heritage but we loved the pictures of animals and what each animal meant to the Indians.

We went to a pow-wow once away to another town. We didn't know what a pow—wow was until we got there. It was cool. There were men, women, and children dressed with feathers on their head dancing and drumming. We loved it. For once mom didn't have to tell us to sit still. We were hypnotized by what we saw.

Mom said we could take a picture with the people. We had to show respect and ask if we could take a picture with them. Every one we asked said "yes." Mom was right. She was like that.

When we left the town she bought us t-shirts about the pow-wow. I loved that shirt. It always calmed me down when I wore it. My sister did not see or feel the difference from her other shirts.

As an adult I learned about feeling and reading energies. My mom always said "it was a gift from creator to feel energy." I guess my sister got a different gift. Mom loved us the same and always knew how to teach each of us. I always knew how smart my mom was. My sister didn't seem to know. She would say words to mom that made her sad. I did not know the words. I remembered when she would tease me and I ripped out her hair. It worked for me. I didn't understand the difference. Later I learned it was about respect and honor. I got it; my sister didn't get it. She said she was the smart one. I could do many things my sister could not do.

## TROUBLE AT SCHOOL

When I had trouble learning my letters at school, my mom would help me cut letters out of sand paper because she said kinetic energy; touching would help me learn the alphabet. I wasn't sure about that word. But if mom said so it was probably true.

Mom would work with me every day learning my letters. She always seemed to know how to teach me. She was smart like that. One day when we were eating breakfast my mom asked my sister to read the letters on the bottle. When my mom saw my face, she knew what I was thinking and feeling—"MY GOD if my mom can't read I will never learn to read." Mom said, "Buddy, I can read but I can't see the very small print." Boy was

I relieved. I never knew how she knew I did not care to ask. One day I took a picture of mom with her reading glasses on just to remind me she could read but not see.

My first book I learned to read was Brown Bear, Brown Bear. I would read it over and over to mom. She was happy. She smiled whenever I was reading Brown Bear, Brown Bear.

# OUR SOLDIERS

When I "crossed over" shaman Dee" said mom and me had special wiring and we could talk to angels. Joey met me with shaman Dee. I knew who he was because I recognized who he was from the manuscript mom sent me when I was stationed in Iraq. I did not know how she knew I was going overseas (Iraq). Dee said the angels told her.

She wrote often. Sometimes her letters and packages were the only things my buddies and I received from home. We called her letters and package "the platoon letters and platoon packages". We passed her letters around over and over. We all laughed at most of her letters. Sometimes it took all of us to figure out her writing. That was no small feat making soldiers laugh on the front line in Iraq. My mom was as good as Bob Hope my buddies would say. I always got the letters back because they were sacred to me. I told Dee when I crossed over that I would feel my mom watching over me and I worried she had "crossed over." She always seemed to know where I was—when she first found out I was in Iraq, I could hear her praying for me and my friends every night. Sometimes I knew mom would wake herself up praying. I knew because I heard her prayers.

She remembered all the times I made her laugh and wrote to me about it. One day she accidentally bought low fat Oreos. My favorite cookies were regular Oreos. My mom said "why not try them." I said at age 5, "it has been my experience that low fat is not as good as the real thing especially cookies." Mom just said okay and gave them to the neighbors. I guess they couldn't tell the difference like I could. Mom wrote a letter about the Oreo cookies and sent a package to me and my buddies in Iraq. She included in the package both low fat Oreos and regular Oreos and asked us to do an experiment and see if we could tell the difference.

## WEEKENDS WITH MOM

Every weekend mom had us with her, we would do something special. One day we went to the Katy Trail to bike. We told mom we could bike to Hartsburg because we did with dad and the other woman. Mom just said "okay." She always believed us because we never lied to her.

After biking for a long time my muscles got so tired and sore. I tried not to but I started crying. My mom immediately noticed my tears. She asked "what's wrong Buddy?" I never said what was wrong but she knew. She locked my sister's bike to the tree (her bike was a Wal-Mart bike). My dad had bought me an expensive one. Mom said she was afraid to leave the expensive one at the tree. She told Lala to ride my bike. I rode on mom's back. She had to petal funny. I liked it. I felt like a bird up there. This was the first time I could experience flying (age 5).

When we got to Hartsburg, mom got us something to eat and called her friend Kitty. Kitty was not at home but Kitty's son

## My Heart Belongs to Mom

Chris came to get my bike and me. Mom told him to wait for Lala to bike back and then meet mom in Jefferson City. She would meet us there. Then she rode with my sister on her seat back to my sister's bike and asked some bicycling friends to escort my sister back to Hartsburg.

My mom then biked back to her jeep because she knew Chris didn't have room for more than 2 bikes. My mom just wanted to be sure we were safe. When we got back to where we started mom got there. She seemed tired and I remember hearing her thinking "I'm bushed." I wasn't sure what that was but I filed it away. I thought I would figure it out someday.

My mom had a jeep wrangler. When she got all 3 bikes loaded on the jeep. It took mom a long time to load our bikes. She liked to fix them so they would not get damaged or broken. She was very careful with things we loved. We got our bikes loaded, buckled up and started to leave I told mom "we could try this next week if she wanted to." She just said "we'll wait a while." I could hear her laughing inside her head. I loved to hear her laugh.

I heard her telling friends the story. I could never understand why they laughed with mom. I figured it was okay because mom would never laugh at us.

One day after she had been biking on the trail, she brought home a t-shirt with an eagle on it. She said a man gave it to her when she asked where he got the shirt because her son loved Eagles. I saw in her mind's eye a sweaty man take off his t-shirt and hand it to mom. I wasn't sure I wanted it. Mom said she would wash the t-shirt and would sleep in it first. That sounded good to me because I liked to feel mother's energy. I didn't call it energy then—it was just a sweet feeling.

# BABYSITTING/BOUNDARIES

It had been a long time before mom went out with friends again. I heard her thinking "can't two 13 year old girls handle a 6 year old boy." One of the babysitters was my mom's friend Kitty's daughter and her friend.

When mom called back to check on us, I answered the phone crying. My mom said "what's wrong Buddy?" I couldn't explain very well. I said "they won't give my boat back." The girls had told me if I didn't take a bath, I couldn't play with my boat. I hated to take baths. Mom would sit by the side of the tub and wash my face, hands, legs, and feet. Then she would tell me, "You wash your personal places." I sure didn't want those girls to see me take a bath. I told you my mom understood boundaries.

She asked if she could talk to Ashley. I said "she's outside." Mom said "well ask her to come to the phone." I said "she can't because I locked her and her friend outside." Mom said "let her in." Then our neighbor started talking to her. She came in the patio door. I heard her say "don't come home." "I will take care of it." Mom told the neighbor to tell Ashley she would give me a bath when she got home. The neighbor knew my mom never went out much. Mom came home before it got dark. I ran out to meet her and saw the neighbor's dad playing catch with his son. Mom seemed sad. I saw them and mom offered to play catch with me. It was fun but mom was still sad. I didn't figure that out for a long time.

## MOVES/ STRESS/NATURAL CONSEQUENCES

I remembered I was always getting angry after we moved from the big house, the rental house, and then to our own house. One day when I was screaming and hitting, mom said, "I love you Buddy but you must learn to control you anger." I was still mad. She held me on the floor with her arms around me. She told me she loved me and wanted me to get control of my temper.

I told her "I hated her." She just said "that's okay if you get control of your temper." It was always about making good choices and bad choices in life. She was like that—I loved her.

One night when she asked if I had any homework, I lied and said "no, I had my homework finished." The next morning I forgot about the lie and said "I forgot to do my homework." She said okay, "let's do it now before we go to school." I couldn't believe it we had to sit down and do my homework before we went to school. Man oh man, my friends had tried that and it worked with their moms. Not my mom.

## SAYING "GOOD-BYE" TO GRANDMA

One night when were going to bed I told mom I didn't want to go to my grandmother's funeral. Mom said "you know how much you love your mom well your dad loved his mother like that." "It would hurt his feelings if you didn't go." I thought about that because I loved my mom a lot. I went to the funeral. I didn't understand why everyone was upset grandma was standing right there by the big box smiling at us. We never saw grandmother again. Maybe she had special wiring too. Maybe the funeral was about saying good—by. I was glad I went.

## TO MY SISTER LISA

Sometimes my sister (eldest) would tease me and swing me back and forth in her arms. She was a lot of fun like that. One day I decided to play with her and said "member Lee, I'm momma's baby." She laughed and said "I know that Buddy."

## ANIMAL STORIES-THE DUCK

One day when my mom and me were going to the lake. You could walk or run around the lake. There was a man in a tan shirt and pants. He was cutting a duck loose from something in the lake. My mom said "some careless fisher man left the fishing string in the lake and the duck got caught." My mom knew I was worried about the duck and asked the man, "My son's worried about the duck." "Will he be okay?" The man said "he would be fine." He was carrying him carefully in is arms. I still wasn't sure. I asked him "if he could still quack?" I could feel my momma laughing inside. I figured the duck was going to be okay or she would not laugh. She loved all animals like me.

## THE BIG TURTLE

One day my mom and I were driving and we saw a huge turtle walking across the road. Mom said "Do you want to stop and get it?" It was a "big turtle." I asked her where we would put the "big turtle?" My mom said, "We can put it in the back seat." I said, "I'm riding in the front seat with you." I had never seen a turtle that big and I wasn't sure about riding in the back seat with a big turtle.

My mom parked the car and we started following the "big turtle." That turtle was really big. I walked with mom following the big turtle for a few minutes. Mom didn't seem to want to pick up the big turtle. When she got close, she never made a move to pick up the big turtle. Finally she said, "Buddy, that turtle seems to know where he is going; maybe we should just leave him alone." I figured he liked nature too like I did. I wasn't too happy to share the back seat with that big turtle anyway.

As I grew older I often thought about that big turtle and wondered if there were any more or if he was the only big turtle in the world. One day when I was at preschool. Everyone called it preschool because they said it wasn't real school. I sure hoped real school was as much fun as preschool. Anyway back to the turtle. I watched in the books for any pictures of "big turtles." I found one, one day. The teacher said it was a "snapping" turtle and if they bit you, he wouldn't turn loose until it thundered. I struggled wondering how mom would drive us home if he "snapped" at her and she had to drag him around until it thundered.

I am sure glad the big turtle had somewhere to go that day.

We never saw that big turtle or any other turtle that big again. I was happy he may have been the only "big turtle" in the world.

# CHRISTMAS

I always loved Christmas. I loved the smell of fresh baked cookies—chocolate chip was another favorite cookie of mine. I was in a Christmas program at the church for preschool. Mom asked me if I had any lines. I thought she said lions. I said,

"No, I have two sheep and a cow." That really made her happy. She liked animals and I figured it was because of that. She told the story to many people and they laughed too. I don't think I figured it out until I was much older. It made me happy that I made so many people happy. It was such a small thing to me.

# RELATIONSHIPS

When I was first talking, I loved purple. My mom bought every boy's shirt she could find that was purple. She could not find too many. I guess I was only boy who liked purple. Mom and I were the only ones who loved purple.

One day when I came home from school mom had found a new purple shirt. I wore it to school the next day. When mom put me to bed the next night she asked if Bethany (my friend) liked my shirt?" I said "yes." She asked me to marry her but I said "no". I wanted to marry Sara because she has shoes like mine. Mom laughed and said "I guess I'll try that next time" (whatever next time meant). Even now when she goes out she still looks for someone with shoes like her shoes. I guess my idea was a good idea. At least I thought so.

# STEP-FAMILIES

One day when I figured out the step-family thing and the different woman was not leaving, I asked mom when she was going to get us a step dad. She said "not until she found someone special enough for us." We must have been really special; she never met anyone to be our step-dad.

As we got older sometimes she would say when we were young she couldn't find any one she liked. Now if she brought someone home, they would hit the road running after they met us and dust wouldn't settle for days. She always laughed. We always knew she was teasing.

I loved to hear my mom laugh.

## RENTAL HOME

When we moved from the big house to the rental house, I was upset and didn't like the changes. I told mom, "I don't have a TV to watch when I eat breakfast like at the big house." My sister and I would eat breakfast at the counter and watch TV. I missed my friend Matt who lived down the street from the big house. Matt's mom called him Mattie. Well my mom fixed that she got a TV on the counter where I could watch TV as I ate breakfast. She asked Mattie's mom if he could spend one Saturday afternoon with us.

We played on the swing set. I told Mattie, "My mom was a marvelous woman-she took the swing set apart, moved it, and put it back together." Later Mattie told his mother and his mother told my mother what I had said to him. She laughed and was happy. I loved to make her happy.

## BIRTHDAY BOAT

One birthday my mom bought me a red remote control boat. Mother had hidden it in the garage in a closet under some rugs. I always knew what mom was thinking like she knew what I was thinking. So it didn't take long to find the boat. I could see it in her mind's eye. It was sure pretty. When I found it, my mom didn't get mad. She just laughed and said, "Only you Buddy."

Most days we would go to the lake that you could walk or run around. I would drive my boat around the lake. My mom said, "Be careful and don't get it in the weeds because I can't go in that yucky green water." I guess she was afraid she might get caught in fishing string like the duck did.

I never got my boat caught because I stayed away from the yucky green water. I was pretty sure mom wouldn't let me go into the yucky green water.

A Mother's Christmas Story

This is one of my favorite Christmas pictures. Thanks to the men who confirmed what I heard in the memorial service about Buddy's tattoo. "My heart belongs to mom." Buddy, "you were the love of my life." You always have my heart along with the children I work with.

# Dollar story-A mother's story

A friend had given you a dollar for your birthday. You talked and talked about what you could buy with your dollar. When you would ask me "can I buy this" or "can I buy that," I would always say "Buddy it is your dollar and you can spend it any way you want to spend it." One day as we were in the checkout line at a super market, you asked what the container of money and picture was about. I said "that little girl has cancer and that money goes to help her." You asked "if you could put you dollar in the container?" I said "it is your dollar and you can choose what you do with it." You quietly put your "treasured dollar" in the container. I don't remember what I said but smiled and patted your back. You were always all heart—everyone's gift from GOD. His most treasured angel to share with us. I love you Buddy. My heart belongs to you. Love mom.

## ADHD

When I was in 2nd or 3rd grade I can't remember. We went to a parent-teachers conference. The teacher was explaining how assignments were made and sent home. My mom wasn't sure what she meant and when my mom asked her, the teacher was very rude to her and said "I can't explain it any other way." Mom seemed worried. I was always worried in that class and was reluctant to answer any questions. If my mom couldn't understand her then I was sure I couldn't either because me and mom were a lot alike. Sometimes I would shake my foot really fast to keep me seated at my desk and not get into trouble.

## SPIRITUAL STORIES-THE JEEP RIDE

One day mom, lala and I were driving down the road. We drove a red jeep wrangler. Lala and I loved that jeep. It felt like we were riding in a bouncing buggy only faster. We always had to be buckled up. My mom was always careful (even back then) obeying the laws and keeping us buckled up. My dad didn't always make us buckle up. It would depend on his mood.

We were bouncing down the road and saw my dad on a bicycle pedaling along on the road. All of a sudden I could hear my mom praying. "Dear GOD, is this a test." I didn't know what kind of test she was talking about. She just kept driving. When we completed our business down the road, we started back on the same road. My dad was pedaling his bicycle along the road. All of a sudden my mom started praying again. I heard her say "God you aren't suppose to give us more than we can handle."

"You sure are pushing you luck today."

I never really understood what the test was back then. She never said and I didn't ask. I don't think Lala heard mom's prayers and thoughts like I did. I was a good listener and liked to know about what made mom happy and sad. She didn't seem to get angry very often. Sometimes she prayed a lot usually about us kids. I remember hearing her pray about us kids. I would hear, "God please don't let him take them away from me." I always knew how much she loved us. I didn't understand who was trying to take us away.

# DIVORCE/LOVE/UNDERSTANDING

One day we asked mom "why she had to go to court all the time?" Once we even went to the sheriff's office to pick up papers that had been served on her. I could never understand how anyone would be mean to my mom. She loved us, all animals, and everyone who knew her. Lala and I were always finding stray dogs and cats to bring home. Mom would feed them; take care of them, take them to the doctor (animal doctor). Sometimes she would put adds in the paper to see if they belonged to anyone. Sometimes people would call and sometimes no one would call.

# My Heart Belongs to Mom

My mom would say "It was important to try because some kids could be missing them." One time someone called and said the dog was their dog but we could keep it. They said "the dog's name was KIKI." We called her Joey's girlfriend because he seemed happier after we got her. She sure was pretty grey and white. She was funny sometimes she would jump on the trampoline with us. Joey never liked to jump on the trampoline, he just liked to watch. Sometimes, I would get off the trampoline and pet him or hug him. He loved to be hugged.

One day Joey got out of the fence with KiKi. Mom immediately grabbed a loaf of bread to entice him back into the fence. He did not understand about traffic and cars so mom was worried about him. She would throw slices of bread into the air and get closer and closer to him until she grabbed him by the collar. I thought I would help mom and began yelling "run Joey run!!" Joey started running. My mom started running down the hill toward the fence gate. All of a sudden Joey began running faster than mom. I think she was barefooted because she had just taken a shower and her hair was still wet.

All of a sudden my mom let go of Joey just before she went head first down the hill. I got Joey in the fence and locked the door. Mom was flying down the hill with mud all over her. She was laughing about being covered in mud. She didn't get mad she just kept laughing and shaking her head. I think it was a "bad choice" Joey.

One day she said we needed to take Joey to the doctor. We had a truck then and she put Joey in the back and she sat in the front seat of the truck. All of a sudden Joey's head pushed through the window. I guess he wanted to ride in front with us. Mom seemed to know Joey could not fit through that window and got in the truck bed with Joey. That was the only way Joey would pull his head out of the window. Mom said "Joey was scared and was shaking all over." Mom tried to calm him down. She had always said "he didn't how to handle traffic." Mom said "Buddy go get the neighbor and see if he can help." I brought the neighbor back. He and mom were friends and they would work in the yard a lot. Mom asked him if he could drive us to the dog doctor. He said "he could."

The neighbor and I rode in the front seat and mom lay in the truck bed holding Joey trying to comfort him. When we got to the doctor's office, mom and I took Joey in to see the doctor. The vet asked if "Joey was dangerous?" Mom said "no, he is a big baby" "he is just scared" as she talked soft to him. The doctor said "you know your dog." The doctor said "what are you feeding him?" He showed us places where he was "pure fat." He said he was only supposed to weigh 60 to 65 pounds. His scale only went up to 150 pounds and he was more than that weight.

Mom said we fed him dog food and whatever we were eating because he liked people food. The birds usually ate his dog food. The doctor said we had to quit feeding him so much. It was not healthy for a dog his age. Mom knew how much he loved to eat and that's why she let him eat what we ate and when we ate. Mom did not know how much he was eating and it was not healthy for him.

She felt bad I could tell. Sometimes when we were eating Joey would come to the kitchen window or dining room door and bark for his share of the food. Mom would fix him a plate of turkey, mashed potatoes, rolls and gravy or whatever we were eating.

## My Heart Belongs to Mom

One time Kitty and her children were having Christmas Dinner with us. My sister started to take Kitty's mashed potatoes and gravy on her plate to give to Joey. I guess Kitty wasn't finished eating her mashed potatoes and gravy. Kitty and my sister were pulling her plate of mashed potatoes and gravy back and forth. Mom said "Lala Kitty wants her mashed potatoes; I will get more for Joey." All was well then. Kitty got her mashed potatoes and gravy and Joey got his mashed potatoes and gravy.

Usually, holidays everyone came to our house because my mom was a good cook. It seemed to always make her happy when friends and relatives came for the holidays. She loved to take pictures especially on holidays. One year, she asked her brother to take pictures. When he took the pictures, he cut off all our heads. When mom saw the pictures she seemed upset. Bill just looked at them and said "I wonder how I did that?" He was living with us for a year and a half. Bill was a lot of fun to be around. Sometimes he would let me help him clean the chimney or work in the yard with him. It was great fun following him around and helping him do odd jobs around the house. Sometimes he would let me hold the tools: hammer, screwdriver, different things with a particular name he knew. I couldn't remember back then, there were so many.

One day Kitty came to the house with Bill. I was watching the Kansas City Chiefs play. I loved the KC Chiefs—my favorite team. Kitty started teasing me about who was going to win. She was for the other team. I was getting upset. Bill took her out of the room and told her to not tease me about the Kansas City Chiefs. It was "too serious for me." Kitty stopped teasing me right away. Bill maybe told her how I would pull my sister's hair out when she teased me.

## A Soldier's Letter to His Mom from the Other Side

Sometimes mom would sit in the kitchen with me while I watched football. I would tell mom what the players were doing and what jobs they had. She always listened "very carefully." She said she could never understand football. She said she couldn't even tell who had the football sometimes.

I liked to watch the hunting/fishing channel. One day I asked mom to watch the hunting show with me. I knew she didn't like to see animals hurt. She said she didn't like to see Bambi hurt. I told her they used targets and they did not show real animals being shot. At least I had not seen any real animal get shot. My mom sat down and the minute she did, a hunter shot a deer with a bow and arrow. I told mom I was sorry. She was not mad. She seemed sad. She never liked to see any animal hurt.

Sometimes when my niece visited, I would tease mom and tell her I was going to tell my niece where McDonald's hamburgers came from. My niece loved the cows that were in the fence by her home in Southwest Missouri. Every day mom said my sister told mom she would feed the cows. She fed those cows—cookies, bread, cereal, or everything her mom had in the kitchen. She loved those cows. I guess she liked animals like mom and I did. I was always just teasing mom about telling her. Mom always knew I was teasing.

My niece would follow me around all the time when she and her mom (my sister) visited. My sister Lee didn't let anyone know I liked playing with her because they said she was a baby. She loved to eat McDonald's hamburgers and French fries. I wondered if she would like the hamburgers so much if she knew they came from cows.

My father was verbally, emotionally and physically abusive to my mom. She blocked much of the abuse from our view. On some level she knew we knew and wanted to protect us. We always knew she cried at night a lot. She would sometimes cry before my next older sister was born. The youngest from another family would ask my mom, "Are you going to leave us?" when she heard my mom crying. My mom would say "not now." She stayed for a long time after she told this sister she would not leave. She was like that my mom. She cared for everyone and every animal she could.

## PICKING MY MOM

Before my sister was born the family had a cocker spaniel puppy. This dog never listened to my mom. My mom would scrape dog dodo every morning out of the room where Rex slept at night. Mom would scrape and bleach out the concrete floor every morning. Sometimes she would ask my dad if they could get a fence for the dog. He always said, "No." My mom would take Rex for a walk often so he could get exercise. Sometimes he would get loose and run all over the neighborhood. Sometimes as many as 7 or 8 kids chased after Rex with my mom. They never caught him until he decided he wanted to be caught or choose to give up. It was pretty funny seeing 7 or 8 kids and a pregnant lady chasing a cocker spaniel puppy. My mom never got angry with Rex.

One time, she took him for a walk on a lease. At some point Rex decided he was not going to walk anymore and lay in the grass. My mom 6 or 7 months pregnant with my sister was carrying Rex home. Two teenage girls saw a pregnant lady carrying a dog and gave her a ride home. I am sure it was pretty funny seeing a 6 or 7 month pregnant lady carrying a cocker spaniel dog. My mom use to say it kept her grounded cleaning dog dodo off concrete every morning. My mom always believed in free will even then. She gave that dog a lot of rope she would say. He never heard the words she said in her mind's eye "bad choice."

I think that was when I first decided I wanted this woman for my mom. She was so kind to everyone and everything she encountered; even Rex who she had to shovel do do out of the unfinished room every day. When she could she would carry him around that way so he wouldn't pooh or whiz on the floor. He was supposed to be pure bread with papers. He was not a smart dog that was for sure.

I think that's when I decided I wanted her for my mom. If she could care for animals like that and children she would be a great mom, a perfect mom, a 100% gentle loving mom. I was right; she was all that and more. I waited for it seemed like a long time to be her baby. One day she was running early in the morning before my dad left for work that was the only time she was free to run—one of the things she loved to do—Run.

She used conceptive (day sponge). I seized my chance. I was going to be the son of the most loving, caring, gentle person in the world—my mom. I loved her for so long before she gave birth to me. I followed her around watching her. She was the most perfect, loving woman in the world. I knew that from watching humans for eons of years in other places. I decided I would incarnate if she could be my mom. I knew she would always protect me. She was all heart. My mom even then I loved her.

My dad once realized her worth. He loved her and placed no one above her. He had bad thoughts but when he was with her "the bad thoughts" seemed to be less. He always cared about money. He was smart, a genius when it came to money. When he was a boy he use to beat up his brother for a quarter and eat dirt for a nickel.

When my mom was little even then she was rescuing lost animals. She once found a kitten with worms in his neck. She never worried she picked up that kitten and took her to her friend who she knew loved animals too. My mom's friend was called the "cat lady." People would dump cats at her house that they did not want. Trink would take care of these animals until they were healthy again. My mom use to go to the basement with Trink to feed the cats. They were everywhere walking on the ledges, on the floor, everywhere. My mom and Trink were never afraid. My mom named the cat she found IKE because Trink liked Ike Eisenhower.

I guess that was where mom learned to take of animals. Some people/most kids wouldn't pick up a kitten with worms in neck. My mom did.

## FISHER PRICE SKATES STORY

One day mom took us to skate at the skating rink. I had Fisher Price skates she had gotten for me. I think I was about 4 years old. I loved to skate. My mom left for a few minutes when she came back, two boys (as tall as my mom) were complaining to the owner about me. My mom walked up and put her arms around in front of me. She could feel my heart beating fast. I told mom those boys started it. She asked what happened to one of the boys. He said I kicked a tooth out which I did kick his tooth out but I was defending myself. I knew my mom believed me. About that time the boys' mother came over to us. She looked at me and said "you boys are twice as big as he is." She appeared to take them by the ears and drag them off. I said again to mom "they started it." Mom seemed to always know the truth when she heard it. The owner said "those boys are bullies to everyone." Mom just shook her head meaning "Bad Choice" for those boys. We never talked about it again. I heard her telling friends the story about the Fisher Price skates and they would laugh with her. I guess they had been bullied before and knew how I felt. (Mom note "I only recently asked Buddy what the boys were teasing him about—he said "they were making fun of my fisher price skates") That makes it even funnier. I laughed again.

## SPECIAL TIMES

Halloween was always a special time for us. We would look at costumes and decide what Lala and I wanted to be. Lala liked to dress up. She would wear her costumes a week before Halloween or as soon as mom bought it for us. She also wore the costume for weeks after Halloween. Mom always let her wear her costume as long as she wanted until she grew tired of wearing it.

I never liked things, masks or paint on my face. Every Halloween, mom would say "Buddy just let me take one picture?" I couldn't say "no" when she asked like that even though I never liked it.

I remember being a clown, puppy, crayon, and ghost. I never looked very happy in those pictures. I always looked like I was about to make my escape or pouting.

The only costume I ever liked was my superman suit. They were really pajamas but I liked to sleep in them so I could dream about flying. One time when we lived in the big house—after my dad and two sisters moved out, mom said we were going to pretend to be Indians and sleep in a tent in our basement. I knew mom had turned the air conditioner off to save money. I guess it was expensive in the big house. Mom said Lala was going to sleep in a t-shirt and under wear and she was going to sleep in a t-shirt and under wear. She said "I would be cooler in a t-shirt and under wear." I still shook my head, "no." My mom said again to me "Lala is sleeping in a t-shirt and under wear and I am sleeping in a t-shirt and under-wear." "You would be cooler." I finally looked at mom and said "I can't fly." Mom said "okay Buddy." I knew when I went to sleep she would take my cape off because she was afraid I would get it twisted and hurt myself. My mom was the best mom in the world, I was sure.

## CHAFTED LIPS

I always had chafed lips because I would get nervous and lick my lips. Mom always wanted to put Vaseline on my lips and mouth to help them heal. I hated it when she did that. She never liked to force me to do anything I didn't want to do. She would explain "it would help my lips to heal."

Sometimes I knew she came in after I went to sleep and put medicine around my mouth and lips because I woke up once. One night when she was putting me to sleep she asked about putting medicine on my lips. I told her "wait until I go to sleep." She just smiled. I could hear her laughing inside her head. I guess she thought I didn't know. I always knew what she was thinking inside—that was the best way I learned right from wrong choices was listening to her thoughts and feelings.

I always knew when something was wrong because I would hear her praying to God. After she went to work, she prayed for the kids she worked with. I guess she wanted them to learn the difference between good and bad choices.

She had something she called a pager. When the families she worked with needed her they would page her and she would call them. She always seemed to care about the families she helped. I always wondered if they could read her thoughts the way I could. I wondered if they knew about the "bad choice" thing that I knew about. My sister never figured out about things that made mom happy—"good choices."

## BOY FRIENDS

Mom had a few boyfriends. They were always trying to get her to marry them. She always said her most important job was raising us kids and taking care of the families she worked with. Some of them didn't understand and would get mad or try to talk her into marrying them. One even asked me if it was okay with me to marry mom. Mom became very upset and told him he should never have said anything to me. I think it was the 'good boundary" thing she talked about. Any way it wasn't long after that she gave his ring back.

He went outside and hammered a door on Joey's doghouse. He was the second man who worked on Joey's dog house when she broke up with them. I later found about "husbands and boyfriends who were in the doghouse." I never figured it out when I was young.

One man told my mom "Joey was going to die someday." She was very upset with him. I think because she knew he was saying it to be mean. Joey didn't die for a long, long time after that man stopped coming over and asking mom out.

Every time we would go to school functions, children and families who knew my mom would come up and talk to her. They sometimes hugged her. She was always kind to everyone she met. I knew she was uncomfortable hugging people in public—kind of like when I didn't want her to hug me in public. I don't think mom wanted to hurt their feelings and let them hug her. I knew they loved my mom. I never worried about her.

One day Lala and I came home from school. There was a man working on the roof of our house. We, of course thought since only men she dated came to the house and he was hammering that she must be dating the roofer. So we asked mom, "Are you dating the roofer?" Mom laughed very hard and said "no, I am not dating the roofer." He had asked her out, she just wouldn't go out with him. She was very particular who she dated because she always said she had two missions in life taking care of us kids and taking care of the families she helped.

## GOOD CHOICES/BAD CHOICES

Sometimes my eldest sister and my niece would come to visit us in Jefferson City. One time they lived with us for a long time. Mom said it was because my sister Lala needed someone who could help take care of Lala so mom could keep working.

I never understood how my sister never figured out about the "bad choices." I knew mom worried about her a lot because of her choices.

One time I remember my sister beat up my mom because she would not let her drive her car she bought for her to drive to school. Mom said "if you don't go to school, you don't drive the car." One time my sister didn't go to school. She needed a change of clothes and parked her car a block away, hoping to sneak home, get a change of clothes and leave. She never figured out how smart my mom was. Mom ran down the street, drove the car home and told my sister she could not drive the car. My sister had made another key and thought she would drive away. My mom just took the key out of her hand and said "no" "you didn't go to school."

My sister started beating my mom up with her Doc Martin shoes mom bought her. My mom never got mad, she just said "no." One of our neighbors (a retired sheriff) saw my sister beating up my mom and called the police. The police put my sister in the back of the police car to take her to the juvenile office. My sister was screaming bad words at my mom. Mom was sad and was crying. The police officer said "she doesn't mean those things." My mom kept crying. She was very sad and kept crying and crying. I hated seeing my mom sad like that.

## EASTER

One Easter my mom bought me a suit like I saw my dad wear sometimes. My mom said "I looked very handsome." I felt stiff and awkward in the suit. I wanted to take it off. Mom said, "Just wear it to Sunday school and I could take it off." My sister loved to wear her new clothes. She never wanted to take them off. I would watch her looking in the mirror at herself. She seemed to like how she looked. I remember when we went to church. Everyone was staring at us smiling. Mom said "it was because we looked so cute." My mom never made me wear that suit again.

I think she loaned it to a neighbor who had a son my size. I wondered if he liked wearing it any more than I did . . . Mom still has the jacket. She smiles whenever she sees it.

## CJ

One day our neighbor's girlfriend gave him a German shepherd puppy. His parents said he couldn't keep her because they didn't have a fence. He was sad and his girlfriend was sad. We told the neighbor we were sure mom would let us keep him at our house. Of course, she said "yes." Mom would say Joey was happy. I guess "he always wanted to be a daddy." He would let that puppy chew on his ears and feet to cut his new teeth. Mom said "the reason CJ was so gentle was because he had Joey as a poppa."

Sometimes when CJ would bit him too hard, Joey would cry and move away from him. He knew about gentleness from mom, I am sure. One day the neighbor (who owned CJ) came to see CJ. The neighbor jumped over the fence. CJ saw him and he started jumping over the fence too. Some times when kids came home from school CJ would jump over the fence and play with them. Joey would always bark at him, "bad choice." He would never jump back in the fence until mom came home and fed him. All the kids in the neighborhood loved CJ.

One day there was a man in another yard swinging a golf club. CJ didn't like it and began barking at him. CJ was probably afraid he would hurt some kid he played with. The man got really mean and complained. Mom had to put CJ on a leash to keep the neighbor from complaining. It was not fun for CJ after that. Everyone began looking for a new home for CJ. The neighbor found a home for CJ in the country. The man had a 100 area farm in the country. He came to our house on a Saturday. He said he had come over when no one was at home and he went to the back yard. CJ and Joey had a "fit." He said he liked him and wanted to take CJ. Mom asked the man "if he could have a donut?" Joey and CJ always ate donuts with us on Saturday morning. The man told my mom "NO, HE'S A POLICE DOG NOW AND HE ONLY EATS DOG FOOD!!!!"

My mom started crying especially when the man put him in a cage to take him home with him. Mom knew he didn't like cages or riding in vehicles. He would throw up when he rode in the car or truck. My mom told the kids in the neighborhood if they wanted to say good-by to CJ they needed to come see him. CJ was leaving for the country. When all the kids CJ played with saw him in the cage in the man's truck, they ran behind him yelling, "By CJ, by CJ!!!" My mom "just cried." She said "she and Joey would miss CJ the most" and they did.

The reason I knew riding in a vehicle upset CJ because he threw up in my mom's truck once. One day mom had an appointment for him at the doctor's office (vet). It had snowed that day and mom ran with him to the doctor's office. She said when they would get to an intersection to cross; CJ would lie down in the snow because he was afraid of cars and trucks. Mom said she had to carry him across ever intersection and road. She said usually people were laughing to see my mom carrying a dog that looked as big as she was across the street. She said she would sometimes say to the people laughing "he's afraid of traffic."

I bet that was pretty funny. My mom only weighed 120 pounds then.

## DALLAS COWBOY STORY

One year mom bought me turtle neck sweaters to wear under my sweat shirts. She always wanted me to be warm. She was like that. She took good care of us. I told her I liked the shirts and she could buy me more. She couldn't find any more like the other ones she bought. She found some that had the Dallas Cowboys on the front of the shirt. I told her I didn't like the Dallas Cowboys. I was four or five. She said "you will have sweat shirts over them and no one will know."

I said "I'll know." She took the shirts back. She knew me and knew I would not wear the shirts. My mom was smart like that.

## SAMMY

My mom went to a friend's house by a lake. She was sitting by a lake. Out of nowhere, this dog jumped in her lap. Did I tell you dogs knew my mom would take care of them? She attracted animals like nats to old bananas. Well, as it turned out the family who owned Sammy was looking for a home for "Sammy." Well, she found one. We only had one dog then Joey. Mom probably figured he was lonesome since CJ left. Sammy was an affectionate, smart dog. She loved kids and some people.

She was a funny dog too. One day when mom left for just a few minutes leaving Sammy home alone. A boyfriend of Lala had sent her roses. Sammy got on the table, knocked over the vase, spilling water and roses all over the floor and table. She had seen one of our cats get on the table before and she thought this was her chance to get on the table. Mom always said "she always wanted to be a cat." Mom came home—there were 18 roses all over the place, muddy paw print on white chair covers and water everywhere. Sammy was lying on top of the table like she was always suppose to be there.

Luckily, for Sammy, mom had a good sense of humor. It was one big mess of water, paw prints, and roses all over and around the table, chairs, and floor. Mom didn't get mad. She just cleaned up the mess and put the roses back in the vase. She never got the paw prints off the chair covers even with taking them out in the sun light to bleach them. She eventually recovered the chairs. She smiles when she thinks of Sammy and the roses.

## JOEY GETTING SICK

Joey began to get sick a lot when he was 16 or 17 years old—people time. He could not squat to go to the bathroom because of his age. A friend of mom's said "he is only alive because of his love for you." Mom decided to help him with his suffering and took him to the doctor. The doctor said "it did not look good." "Joey was tired."

When Joey died, me and my sister left home, mom decided to move to the town where she was working. Mom listed Sammy in the newspapers to interview people to see if they were kind people and would take care of Sammy like we did. Mom found several homes but the one she decided would be best for Sammy was a home in the country. She was going to be a companion dog for a disabled man in a wheel chair. They lived on a big farm in the country.

Sammy would be able to run free. Mom had to be careful in town because there were leash laws where dogs had to be hooked up or in a fence. One day Sammy was on the porch with mom and suddenly Sammy started walking with the mail man. My mom said, "don't worry she won't bite." The mail man said "I know she walks with me every day." Sometimes, we called her "Houdini" dog because we never knew how she got in and out of the fence. Did I tell you she was smart? After mom found a home for Sammy she would call and check if Sammy was okay. The new people said "she was the best dog they ever had." She would walk the mom to the car every day and meet her at the car every evening when she came home from work. During the day she stayed right by her husband who was confined to a wheel chair. Even though Sammy had the run of the farm, she chose to take care of her master.

I know now animals especially dogs take care of people the way they were cared for. Sammy understood unconditional love and caring. Some children don't receive the love and care our animals received from us.

I think that is why my mother works with children. She is especially committed to children who no one loves. She always said "when you feel love, you will always know what it feels like to be loved." Then you will understand when you are being mistreated. Everyone will always choose love.

# SAYING GOOD BYE TO A FRIEND

We had a lot of cats. Mom taught us about saying good-bye to someone or an animal we loved. Someone had poised one of our cats. She came home to die. Mom said we should bury her. She dug a hole under a tree, wrapped a blanket around the cat and buried her. We put a cross on her grave. My mom, sister, a neighbor and me held hands and my mom said a prayer asking GOD to welcome this animal home. My neighbor and I sort of laughed—we weren't sure if animals went to heaven. When I crossed over Grandfather Dee, my mom's friend Olga, and Joey met me. Joey was young, strong, and beautiful. He said "he took care of mom now the way she took care of the children and animals." In addition, when he saw an animal (be they deer, cows, horses, dog, cats. sheep), he took them home. All kinds of animals Joey helped them to go home and they usually choose to come back to mom's house.

Joey said he went to sleep. Mom held his head until his body died. He said he was very sick, old and couldn't go to the bathroom without falling. My mom took him to heaven. My mom always told us "all dogs go to heaven." My mom said that before the movie came out about all dogs go to heaven.

When we lived in the big house, my oldest sister was upset because her dog Tonka died. My sister cried and cried about Tonka. My mom said maybe "grandma needed Tonka in heaven." My sister got mad and said "Dog don't go to heaven!" Mom left the advertisement for the movie on the counter for my sister to read when she came home from work. Mom wanted her to see someone else believed "all dogs go to heaven."

When my niece (about age 12) came to visit my mom, she went home and asked her mom "Isn't Nana's old dog Joey dead?" Her mom said "yes a long time ago." My niece said "I felt that dog jump in the bed with us every night." My niece had a gift from GOD, "she could see ghosts and spirits." She told her mom "she saw cats and dogs roaming around Nana's house." I bet my sister believes "all dogs go to heaven now." After that when my mom's house got too crowded Joey started taking animals to my sister's house.

Joey said he never brought snakes, reptiles, and spiders because my mom was afraid of them . . . Even Joey understood "good boundaries."

You see when I crossed over to heaven; I learned just how special my mom was from Dee, Olga and Joey (Olga & Dee were close friends of my mom when they were alive). She came into many, many life times as an abused child so when this lifetime came, she would know just what to do to take the lost children home. Olga and Dee said "because children who have been mistreated in any lifetime don't always know about angels and a loving GOD." All they have ever known was sadness and suffering. God gave my mom a special gift to be able to help these children because of what she endured through many lifetimes. Dee said "it had been foretold many eons ago my mom Echata (The One Whom Many Children Love) would help the lost children to go home."

Dee said she finished the job 30 years ahead of time. Now, I know why children and animals always loved her so much. She lived the longest this lifetime she ever lived because of the abuse she endured in past lives. Dee said loosing me was the most difficult thing she ever experienced in any lifetime. She is sad but someday she will see me again. I will be waiting for her.

Mom often would ask GOD why she could never see the children she took home. One of her co-workers sent her an e-mail of children who had been abused saying "We speak for those who can't." My mom could only look at one or two pictures. She told the friend she was glad she was sending the e-mail out to others. She just couldn't look at them. This was the first time she realized why God did not let her see the children she took home. My mom was all heart and if she would see these children it would have broken her heart.

I never told my mom about some of the skydiving. I did jump off bridges, towers, tall buildings, cliffs and other things. Grandfather Dee said "mom would look at the U-tube videos on the internet just to see my face." I'm sorry mom for not seeing you again before I left this world. I knew how much I always missed you but I never realized how much you missed me. All the things I learned about love were from you. I was 15 when I went to live with my dad in Arizona. By then my abilities to see truth from lies were well developed.

I know when I was young and I would spend the first 10 days of the month with dad. Then when I would come home to you for the rest of the month, I would always be sick the first day home and not go to school. You always let me stay home with you. You use to say "I had mommy-itis." By the next day spending a day home alone with you, I always felt better and could go back to school.

I never understood what "mommy-itis" meant until I moved to Arizona with my dad in 2001. I was 15 years old. I only got to see you a few days at Christmas and maybe a week in the summer if I was lucky. I didn't understand until I crossed over why you allowed this—you thought it was what I wanted. You always kept joint custody in Missouri hoping I would change my mind. I never knew "no one told me."

I discovered what "Mommy-itis" was the first month I didn't see you. I missed your understanding and sweet nature. There was no one in the world like you. You always said "I was special." It was very difficult for me living so far away from you. My relationship with my dad and the other woman was strained often. I began to understand what mattered most to them—it was always about money. I began praying too. Sometimes I used drugs to numb the feelings and thoughts I heard from them and other people.

Dee said it was difficult for me to understand my gifts then. I became more and more depressed. Sometimes, I would do anything just to keep going. After being sent to a drug rehab unit, I decided I would join the Army as soon as possible. I felt anything would be better than the life I was living. Dee said "I just didn't understand depression and how to help myself."

Dee said "my mom went to an army recruiter and the office was closed then she went to a Navy recruiter and told them her son had joined the Army. "She said "she had joint custody in Missouri." She thought I was 17 not 18 when I joined the Army. She was always bad at remembering my age. It was her friend (Linda) who was an accountant who figured out my age when she and her husband were trying to console my mom.

My mom started writing me when I was in boot camp from talking to the Navy recruiter. My mom was pretty courageous when it came to her children. She wrote often to me. When I was sent to Iraq, her letters started coming back that I was not at Fort Hood. I did send my mom a mother's day card and a picture of me in uniform from boot camp. I found out later she would look at that picture and pray for me all the time.

When her letters started coming back she wrote to the US government asking for my new address so she could start writing me. Mom received a reply back within a week of sending the letter. Dee said the Army knew a sincere letter when they read it. My mom started writing and sending packages right away. She sent me all the stuff she knew I loved Oreo cookies, Skittles, chocolate chip cookies (homemade). It was probably more expensive to send the stuff than send money to buy it. I found out what "it is the thought that counts" meant. My buddies and I loved her packages and letters. They said they never knew anyone like her. They never met her and loved her.

When I crossed over some of my friends who were stuck over there (not knowing the way home) met her. The first night I had crossed over mom and I would go to the Middle East and started bringing them home. I always appeared in uniform so they always recognized me. My mom was always herself. She was the real angel not me. She always said "I was her gift from God." The meaning of Matthew—my middle name.

I never knew until I crossed over how mean my father was to her. She never once told me. She was a good mom—all heart. I understood what she meant when she would pray to God "please God, don't let him take them away from me."

Dee said many men who were abusive would tell their wives "if they ever left they would never see their children again." He said "many women are afraid to leave for this reason." Dee said "my mom left because she did not want us to see the way he treated her." I never knew. Dee said "she always advocates for the children when the parents are going through a divorce battle." She will tell them if they were upset for them to go outside away from the children scream, yell, or howl at the moon if it helped. Always, show the mom the same respect they did when they were together. She always praised parents who came in and said they always wanted to do the right thing for their children. Some parents said and did do the right thing. Many parents tried to do the right thing. Dee said they all remembered what she said because they recognized wisdom when they heard it. He said it was one of her standard speeches.

I was always proud of my mom. I was especially proud when I crossed over and realized how much she had endured to keep us safe. I understood about free will. When I became an adolescent she never knew how hard it was not seeing her as often as I needed to. Dee said "my mom always understood I needed to learn about the business world." She also knew she could not tell me about those things. One of the many reasons me and my sister choose to have my mom and my dad as parents was because we would learn about things of the heart from one parent and love of material things from the other parent. I learned that lesson well.

I remember when I was 4 or 5 mom had tied big yellow ribbons on the front door wreaths. When she was putting me to bed I asked her "why she did that?" She said "the yellow ribbons represented love and prayers for the soldiers and to bring the soldiers home safe." I didn't understand so I said "why don't we just get in the car and go get them." My mom smiled and "I could feel her laughing inside her head" so I knew it was not an option to get in the car and go get them or she wouldn't laugh. I loved to make my mom happy.

Well mom, we're bringing those soldiers home. Just the way you wanted—they come home with love and prayers. My mom sent me a picture of herself holding a big cardboard yellow ribbon which read "SUPPORT OUR TROOPS." All my buddies loved the letter and picture. She told me the story about the yellow ribbons in her letter.

When I came home from the first trip overseas somehow my mom knew. The angels told her "I was hurting." She had written a letter to my commanding officer saying "she could help me." I'm sorry I believed the lies I was told about your letter. I called and left you a mean message about writing your boss about your work. I had severe PTSD and no one knew but the one person who didn't get to see me MY MOM. I successfully hide it from everyone else.

I went back to help my buddies. Many were afraid. They asked me "how I was always so brave?" I said "I do what I heard my mom do PRAY-PRAY-PRAY." I went back overseas three times. I lied to my dad about one trip. He was having a hard time with my being gone. I never knew until I crossed over how hard he had made it for mom to keep us. He made fun of our heritage "Native American". She even took the Sacred Animal Path cards to court once. He made fun of her strong belief in Angels, her innate goodness. She even cried for him in court. He realized what he had lost whenever he would see her and especially after I crossed over seeing her. She always had a light around her. Anyone could see that light.

I asked her to help my buddies (friends in Arizona) after the memorial service. They were hurting and blamed themselves for my accident. When she was at the memorial service I heard her thinking "I wonder what Buddy's tattoo says." I told her "my heart belongs to mom."

I wanted her to know if anything happened to me she would always know how much I loved her. I wanted her to know I was not angry at her for writing my army boss. She never knew how hard it was for me. I was better than most who came home. Very few people knew—only my dearest and closest friends knew what I struggled with from being in the Army. It made me sad when I came home and saw the unfeeling, uncaring people who we saw in airports and home. They never knew how hard their soldiers/brothers worked for them or the high price they paid. I went back three times to help my brothers until I had an injury to my hand. I was given an honorable discharge. I received other awards. I am sure my dad never told my mom about them. I never knew he tried to block her from communicating with me.

He didn't know my mom. He never knew she had friends in high places (God and the angels); they could not be intimidated by wealth and power. Mom, go ahead and write the Army about me. I want you to know. I tried to get through to dad. He wasn't listening to me or he just couldn't listen to his heart.

When my mom met my buddies I had the accident with—at least one friend. One had already left the building. She figured out he was already talking to me because someone told her he was deaf. She knew immediately we had a lot in common now. He and I communicated quiet well together before the accident and after the accident. He was okay about everything and knew I was happy. She communicates like that with many of the children she works with professionally. Many times the children had injuries/traumas that were preverbal and were unspeakable. Dee said "God gave her gift to to zap that memory out of their minds—usually it was symbolic meanings." Dee always wanted her to complete a study comparing children she worked with and other counselors. He said anyone who could read brain feedback could see how their brain structure changed after my mom worked with them.

Mom would never do this because she never wanted to bring attention to herself. It was enough for her to know God knew. Dee said "she never told anyone but her cousin Silver Star." There were often times people who were jealous of my mom and talked bad about her. She never stopped doing what she knew in her heart was right. It was always about the kids Dee said.

I didn't know a lot about my mom's adult life. She always focused on us and what we needed. When she started doing the job she does now, things the children would say and do would trigger memories about us. She always remembered and laughed. She always knew what the best intervention was to help them just like with me and my sister.

Dee said "she never missed not then and not now." Dee said "mom had often begged Creator to let her come home." God would say "just a little long—remember you were going to do this or that."

Dee said "she use to have a lot of helpers (children, boys, and girls of all ages to help-angel children)." She looked like the piped piper from over here (heaven). Dee said she got the majority/largest group of children home 30 years early. Dee said eleven children went to reincarnate. She still had two helpers Sara and

Sassy. When she felt the others leaving even though she could not see them she became depressed. She is able to feel many things Dee said.

One time when she was driving home and a baby bird fell out of his nest trying to fly she heard the angels telling her to go to her back yard. She didn't touch the bird just beamed Reike light at the bird. It didn't take long and he was ready to fly. It is true what the Bible says "God hears the smallest sparrow fall."

Dee said this was my mom's master life time. This was the longest lifetime she had lived 63 years. Dee said my mom and God had a special relationship. One time when she was flying back from seeing her grandchildren in Florida, God chose to talk to her through an elderly black man she was sitting by on the plane. My mom could feel he was there and wanted to put her head on his shoulder. Of course, she didn't—she knew about "good boundaries." She asked God about me. He winked and said "he'll be okay." I'm glad he gave her that message years ago. She remembered what he said when I had the accident.

I was okay. I'm okay now. I worry about you. You are so sad. I wish I could take the sadness away. Dee said it was how bereavement worked—no one could take it away. I know you still pray and take care of children and animals. I know you gave up the dream to see me again when I walked this earth. If I had known how much and how hard it would be for you that is one thing I would have changed. I just thought it would be easier for you. I changed a lot in the Army. My close friend who spoke at the Memorial Service said "I was wise beyond my years."

I knew many things that God wanted me to see and know. I was his messenger. He does not like the fighting among brothers here or anywhere else in the world. I knew you had your work to do also. I had my work I had to complete before I could go home.

God hates cruelty of any kind, any lies, and any untruths, anything mean or uncaring. He said if there was a price tag on it then it was not worth fighting over. He said "you always understood that from an early age." When people become so mixed up in material things they lose sight of what is really of value: Love, human life, caring about your fellow man, taking care of your brother.

Dee told me the story once when someone asked you "if you got a lot of money for taking lost souls home?" You just laughed and said "I don't charge God." God laughed a lot about that one—a little esoterical humor.

You father Wa-sha-nu said in a message he sent you "he would help you in cleaning and caring for mother earth. "He said "you thought he meant composting not putting portals to clean mother earth of negativity." I wish you could go all over the world making portals for God—his gift to you. Dee said the angels called them "the bathroom portals" because that is where you usually go so people don't look at you strange. Good Boundaries Mom.

You knew God gave you permission and no one else mattered. God loves you mom, the angels love you, the animals love you, all the children and people you took home love you. The children you help everyday love you. My heart will always belong to you mom. It is like you said once at my confirmation when I was 12 years old. The teacher at the church said she was sorry she didn't know you were there and did not acknowledge you. You said "Buddy knows who his mom is." I remember when you asked me about going back to your maiden name; I said "I know who my mom is." You smiled.

I am sorry I never met Leann. If you love her, I am sure I would love her. I found out about your dream when I crossed over— the dream of me meeting Leann, falling in love with each other, getting married and living close to you. You have good taste. Leann knew how much you cared about her to match make her with your son. I was happy to see all the prayers and happy thoughts about you after I crossed over. Dee said "God smiled too." Dee said you don't always realize the love from others. God sent you 11 owls on one birthday as a Happy Birthday sign. You just counted them, smiled and said "thank you." You never told many people because sometimes you know they think "you are eccentric" but God knows you and that is all that counts to you.

Sis,

I wish you could have my gift for just one day to see truth from lies. Look into your heart you will see the truth. Mom would never hurt or abuse a child. When I was a young boy, dad told me "mom didn't love me." I went home and asked her about what he said. She became very quiet and sad. She showed me picture after picture of me and mom. She would say "does this look like a mom who doesn't love her baby." I knew truth even then.

Your brother

Buddy

## SAGE STORY

I remember mom would burn something in a pan and would walk around every room and closet with this smoking stuff. She said "it would get rid of negativity." We didn't understand the word until she explained it to us. She said it would take away any bad thoughts or actions in our home.

I asked why other mothers didn't do that because our home was always happy. When I got older I found out it was sage and the Indians burned it for the same reason my mom did. I always wondered if she knew about sage before the Indians knew about sage.

I assumed it was mom because I knew how smart she was.


## BUMPER BEDS

Mom bought me bunk beds. I loved those bunk beds. I called them bumper beds. Mom would laugh when I said that and tell other people. One night when I was sleeping on the top bunk, I fell out of bed. I didn't wake up until mom came in to my bedroom and put me in the bottom bunk for the rest of the night.

She was like that—she was the best mom ever.

One day mom got a hammock and I tied it in the bottom bunk and I slept in it. It was pretty cool and I never fell out of it.

One day mom decided I needed a big boy room not the one I was in or at least different wall paper. I loved the Miami Dolphins. She painted my room a soft turquoise and put a border of the Miami Dolphins all around the room.

I told mom "it was the best." "My dad could not do something like this." She said, "He would hire someone to do it." Mom doing it made it special. I knew she put love into everything she did for us kids. I could feel that love.

## KANSAS CITY CHIEFS' S QUARTERBACK

Mom would play football, baseball, ride bikes, and skate with us kids. One day after Joe Montana left the Chiefs. The Chiefs were my favorite football team. I told mom I thought she should marry the new quarter back for the KC Chiefs.

She just laughed and said she figured he had plenty of girlfriends. She said she appreciated my feeling he would go out with her. I could not figure it out. I knew mom was smart, caring, a hard worker, and pretty. I knew if he just met her he would love her like we did.

She never looked him up.

# A MOTHER'S PRAYER

During my darkest moments, I wrote this poem crying. Friends wanted me to include it in the book.

He was my gift from GOD and he was called home. I will never hold him,

I will never laugh with him, and know and feel the most wonder of GOD

I WANT TO RUN THROUGH THE STREETS SCREAMING MY SON IS DEAD

I have lost others—my mother, my father, my grandparents, my brother, many friends. Many I have loved. BUT NONE CAN COMPARE TO THE LOSS OF MY SON.

I WANT TO RUN THE STREETS SCREAMING MY SON IS DEAD

Can't you hear me? Can't you feel my pain and sorrow? I use to pray when he was young, please GOD take me home if you take him. Now he is gone and how can I go on? What is there for me to look forward to—all my hopes and dreams are lost and gone.

I WANT TO RUN THROUGH THE STREETS SCREAMING MY SON IS DEAD

Please GOD gives me the strength to go on. Give me strength I can give to others—about love, loss, grief and sorrow. Only those who have experienced the loss of a child know the depth of my sorrow.

My life goes on; other people's lives go on. How do they go on? He was so kind, sensitive, so true and courageous. He was all those things to me and he became all those things to those who loved him.

Will my burdens, my loss ever lighten? It is hard to imagine not feeling this pain and sorrow. How do others survive losing a child? Tell me how others survive the loss and keep going? I don't know. He talks to me often saying "mom it will get better." Dee tells me "I can't take your sorrow away." Will the sorrow ever diminish?

Not for now

Maybe never

I pray it gets better with each passing day.

Please God please grant me this prayer that I pray. I want to come home to be with my son. Please lift this burden off my heart and other mothers who want to run through the streets screaming my son is dead.

File Name is "Reading with d. Dec. 15. Buddy's Message"

Sandy speaks:

1. Thank the Color Guard for their kindness. "I know my son would have been proud."

2. The Minister

3. The friend

4. The Prosecuting Attorney (Buddy's Jump partner); "Thank you for letting me know Darrell, The Man. I had not seen him for many years face to face. I always had faith that God was taking care of him the way I always took care of him.

5. M, thank him for telling me the message "My Heart belongs to MOM" that was Buddy's way of letting me know (if anything ever happened to him).

That . . . When he was in Iraq, she prayed for him, She prayed for every man in Iraq.

He wanted to protect me, let me do my work because he was doing his work, work Creator wanted him to do.

And, when he was finished, he felt safe to go.

And, all those he loved, and loved him, he'll always remember.

He told me, he said, he and I were telepathic.

And, he knew I prayed a lot.

Then, when he didn't see me, he started missing me, and then he started praying.

Telepathically, he heard me praying. He prayed to God and I prayed to God.

_____ ~ shift ~_____

[Buddy comes in through Shaman d:]

"And God let me know it was alright. And, my Mom was alright, "Love goes on forever. Love never ends."

She taught me that.

She was a special Mom. And no one can ever, ever take that away.

She taught me to "Be True to Myself."

She taught me to "Love Others no matter how they treat you."

And, "Walk away as often as you can when you know they're wrong and they know they're wrong."

"Fight for what you believe in."

And, what I said many years ago when she took down the swing set,

"She was a Marvelous Woman. She could take that swing set apart.

And I told my friend and he told his mother, "She's a Marvelous Woman."

And, I'm going to watch out over her and take care of her the way she has taken care of me.

# A Soldier's Letter to His Mom from the Other Side

I may not have been face to face.

But the Love she gave me and the things she taught me carried me through all my life.

When I cared about people (I tried not to be intrusive), I could sometimes read their thoughts, but they always knew I was there when they needed me.

My Mom taught me that.

It was not just 7 generations. It was ALL generations. (She never understood that '7 generations'.)

She could turn around, and look back, and know,

"She was a Marvelous Woman . . . EVERY GENERATION.

[Grandfather d says, "This is coming through Shaman d.]

"I didn't want my Mother to go through any more pain.

"Tell Star to tell her, "FLY FREE WITH ME."

"The Children still need her to teach and love them and show them the way.

My Mother is a Marvelous Woman.

She's still a Marvelous Woman

And, . . . she'll always have My Heart.

Tell Sandy, he reminded me of my Mom. He was so tender and sweet.

I knew, once my friends met her, they would love her. They would feel our Love of Mankind and All Things Living. It didn't matter if Children were black or white. And any Animal, she took care of it till she found a good home, just like she does the kids, until they are free to fly home, where, Love Goes On Forever. Thank you for supporting and loving my Mom because I know it's very hard to give me up.

She was crying. We never knew the struggle she went through. We knew she was sad, was hurting and was angry, and we heard her crying, but we never knew why. One day she was talking on the phone to my dad, then, after that, she didn't talk to him anymore. Then she hadn't talked to him for five years.

Now, she has more reasons to be happy, and I want my friends to be happy, too. HOW I LOVED THEM!

And, I knew how much THEY LOVED ME.

Thank you, Star, for protecting my Mom and keeping her safe.

I am Proud of Lisa.

I am Proud of Shelby.

All the way down and back.

And, believe me, it was *"quite a mission."*

You didn't fail, any of you.

So, all the Generations back,

They send Love to you, and they send Love to my Sisters.

Good-Bye, Friends.

Good-bye, Brothers.

Good-Bye, Sisters.

I'll see you in the Skies.

BUDDY,

"MY HEART BELONGS TO MOM."

~ End Message, 1:11pm

~ 12-15-2009

\* \* \* \* \* \*

Echata said "And then put, please put the REIKI PRAYER on there."

## The REIKI (Christ Light) Prayer

As I am healed,

My Friend is healed.


As My Friend is healed,

WE are healed.


As WE are healed,

Mother Earth is healed.


As MOTHER EARTH is healed,

The Galaxy is healed.


As the GALAXY is healed,

Spirit is healed.

**As SPIRIT is healed,**

**The Infinite Vibration**

**Of JOY**

**Is born.**

\* \* \* \* \* \* \*

*O sa da dv* ~ All is Good (in Cherokee Star Language)

*Mitakuye Oyasin* ~ We Are All Related (Dakota Star Language for "We Are ONE."

Love, Light, Peace, UNITY, Harmony, Truth, and FREEDOM,

SilverStar

# Teachings of Shaman d

This is the manuscript Echata sent to her son in Iraq.
It was read and loved by many soldiers.

by *Grandmother SilverStar* and
*The One Whom Many Children Love*

# Teachings of Shaman d

by *Grandmother SilverStar, Notlvsi Adelv Unega,*
and *The One Whom Many Children Love, E cha ta*

First printing May 2004

*When I walked this Earth*

*I was a Guardian.*

*I was a Soldier.*

*I was a Protector.*

*I was a Knight.*

Throughout my life many aspects came into play. I worked hard in these roles. I became a Father and a Provider, a Teacher and a Healer, a Mystic and a Shaman.

The healing came out of the providing, the giving, and the loving. The healing came as a piece from that. All my life, I devoured readings about mystical aspects of life. The essence of who I was on this plane when I walked this Earth evolved over many years, many experiences, and many teachings. It took a great deal of hard hard work.

All those aspects, all of those things I worked on and developed, I took with me when I crossed over. They are *still* a part of who I am. They cannot be separated. When we come in (to the Earth plane) and work very hard to become the best person we can become, to become that person that Creator knows we can become, it is **there**, it is anchored in, it is grounded in. **And we take it with us!**

And that's a lesson we don't have to learn again. That's a road we do not have to go down again. It's just as many of the things we are clearing out now, they are cleared out *for good*.

If I choose to incarnate again, and I may someday—with *my beloved—I will come back in with the *full knowledge* of

---

* [Here d shares his amazing experience of finding his soul mate after he crossed over, *"If you would like to share about meeting my soul mate when I crossed over and the beauty of that! please feel free to. For I want you to know that if your Prince Charming doesn't come along, he may be waiting for you over here. The last 30, 40 years of my life was very lonely. When I was not teaching, when I was not visiting my daughter, who, as you know, was suffering from a severe mental illness, I was alone. I was alone for pretty much three-fourths*

*what I possess now.* I will not come in with things shielded from me. I will come in **knowing who I am,** *who I have* **always** *been in my life.*

There are many who come into this lifetime *unaware* of *who they are* or *who they've been* or *who they are going to become.* Many come in and they are shielded. This knowledge is not disclosed to them. They work hard to understand who they are as people, as individuals, as spiritual entities. And they strive to develop all aspects of their personality, much like the archetypes that are presented in the book *Sacred Contracts.* (*Sacred Contracts, Awakening your Divine Potential.* Copyright 2001. Harmony Books. New York, New York.)

We come in *without* the clear knowing of who we are and of what we are to become. In that way, we are open to many, many possibilities. There is an astrological wheel of opportunities, of *windows* of opportunities, of these certain aspects. Then you have an opportunity to make *certain* choices, *certain* changes, *certain* advances, certain *quantum leaps* in your life. And, if you make that **right choice,** if you've moved along in each different section of this wheel, it's almost like a **quantum leap** forward in

---

*of my life. When I crossed over I met this incredible, incredibly beautiful being who just lit up my life! All of my experiences in all of my lifetimes could not begin to equal the experience and the love and the sharing and the giving that I am experiencing at this time with this one known as Olga—Olgita. She was alone much of her life. She was ill most of her life. There were very few who were there for her, who cared for her, who loved her, who provided for her. And this one, The One Whom Many Children Love, was one of those who loved and cared for her. Know that all my time alone was worth waiting for. This one is everything I could ever want in a soul mate. I am fortunate to be part of this group of helpers for Creator."]*

time. ***Good choices*** progress you *farther* and *quicker* up the road, developing your spiritual life, opening your*self* up to the Great Spirit of the Universe—of *all* Universes, not just this Universe, *all* Universes.

There are certain points on the astrological chart, this Wheel of Life for the entity, the individual, and his relationship to humanity. Then there are additional points in these astrological charts for humanity, for individuals. Creator makes these astrological charts for humanity, for the individual. There's such a range of opportunities, of things that they can accomplish in their life—if they choose to, *if they choose to.*

\*\*Creator experiences those highs, those lows of ***every single entity*** on this Sphere, in this Universe, ***every single person*** in

---

\*\*  One time she said to me, *"Now, I understand how I help the families, the people I work with in counseling, because I know how it feels when I'm with you, d."* And it was truly one of the most beautiful moments that I was gifted with from her. She was saying, *"I understand how I make others feel because when I'm with you, d, you make me feel loved and special."*

You (SilverStar) have watched your sons J. and G. evolve over the years. And you've seen them go down various paths—sometimes good paths, sometimes not-so-good paths. You always knew they would get back **on**, get back **on that path**, that **Path of Spirit.**
This is what Creator wants for us. That is what you want for your children. *"So, As."* Yes, *"As above, so below."* You *know* where they need to be. You do not have to tell them. It is good. It is not as though you have to have this, *"Hello! Wake up call."* The fact remains: The **choice** is there. When you talked to your brother K., the **choice** was there. He *made* the **right choice.** He made the right decision. He didn't have to. He could have continued

this World, **every single Planet, and every single Star**. In a very miniature comparison, it is as a mother knows where her children and grandchildren are. She knows where they are *emotionally*. She knows *where they are* in their (physical) development. She knows how they're getting along. It is the same with Creator. This comparison is a very *scaled down* understanding of how Creator works with us. Just as we want the very *best*, the very most *love*, and the very most of *good things* to come into the lives of our children and grandchildren and great-great grandchildren, Creator wants that for us.

---

on his path of poor choices. But, he changed. He made the **right decision, the right choice**.

Just like *The One Whom Many Children Love, E cha ta,* told her granddaughter in the Dreamtime, "S., *I'm not happy with the way you've been treating your mother. It's not nice. I love your mother. I love you. I want you to work hard to help your mother. She's not well. She needs your help. She needs your support.*" That is where *The One Whom Many Children Love* talks to her grandchildren—in the Dreamtime.

(We can verbally communicate. We can write. We can communicate in the Dreamtime. It is our choice. There are many options. But *instinctively* we *know* the best way to approach an individual. Just as Olga knew it was best to approach L. in the Dreamtime. She talked to L. in the Dreamtime, and L. listened, and she made changes *immediately*.)

Creator gives us these messages like this, too, in different ways, for different causes. We *know* what's important. Each one is as important as the other. Your job is *just* as valuable as any other individual's decision to do Creator's work. It makes Him happy. It makes Him smile and sing when we continue to **make good choices**, continue to **do what is right** and **good** and **wonderful**. Just as *we* smile and sing when our own children make **good and right choices**.

And it as if we lived for 127 years, you continue to live forever without taking a respite.

We would have many generations who come back, many many many many generations come back. We cannot change the love we felt for this individual or the other child or the other grandson or the other grandchild or the great-great-great-great-great-great-great grandchild. When we love someone, when we care for them, it's as if a piece goes throughout eternity. The **LOVE**, the **connection**, the **LOVE** you *feel* for your child, there will be a part of you—your Higher Self—that *knows* everyone you have ever loved or who loved you. **LOVE** goes on—without end. **LOVE is INFINITE**. Other things fall away—hard feelings or disappointment, but the **LOVE** . . . when you love someone, that **LOVE is FOREVER**. That **LOVE will be FOREVER**. It exists in **INFINITY**.

You *know* what your children are capable of. It's as if they are *a part of you*. They are a part of us, because we are a *spark* from God when He creates us. Then when we have children, there is that *spark* from God, **and** there is also the *spark* that goes on from us to the child, especially that **LOVE**. If there is great **LOVE** there will always **be** that *special spark* within the Children.

For example, no matter if she come back one hundred years from now, the **LOVE** that *The One Whom Many Children Love, E cha ta,* has shown to her children will recognize her; that **LOVE** will recognize her a million years from now. Because that

**LOVE** she gives is **REAL**. And it's tangible. And the children *know* that they are

**LOVED**. They **know** they are **LOVED**. And, when they feel that **LOVE** from her, they understand what it's like to be **LOVED by Creator.**

# Good Choices

There was a story about a young man. His mother had been incarcerated. He had been abused—sexually and emotionally and physically. He spent his youth in foster homes. Then, for a time, he lived on the streets. Then he finally found a way. A social worker took him to a halfway house. Then he met a teacher, a healer, a naval officer, who was a counselor for young men. The young man had an anger problem, very explosive. The counselor helped this young man to look at his life, to understand what happened, to understand what caused the anger. The young man cleared out, cleared away all of those past negative patterns The counselor helped him find a new identity—an identity that he was loved and that he was cared about and that he was a Divine Child of Creator.

(This is exactly what *The One Whom Many Children Love* does in her practice, in her work with the children. She gives them a new identity of being *loved* and *valued* and *cared about*.)

As it turned out, the young man did meet his mother. He said to her, "*Why did you not find me? Why did you not look for me? I thought of you every day. I imagined where you were and what it was like for you.*" Then he said, "*I didn't do drugs. I work very hard. I'm honest. I'm responsible. I'm a good person. I try to do the right thing. I was mistreated but, I always tried to do right. I always tried to be a good man, a good person.*"

And he kissed her on the cheek. And he said, "*Good-bye.*" And she sat there and cried because she *knew* she had lost him because of the bitterness. She always had the choice to help this son that she had abandoned or to turn her back to him. And she chose to turn her back to him. In addition, when she abandoned him she did not tell the father's family. They had not been aware of his existence. When he found his father's family, they welcomed him with open arms. Even though he had been abandoned, throughout his life, the young man had held that fierce pride in him that kept him *exactly where he needed to be.* He *walked* his path. He *talked* his path. He *walked* and *talked* his path. He was a Warrior of the Light. [This story has been made into a movie called *"The Antoine Fisher Story."*]

And **you** *know*. **You** have your *inner knowing* of where you need to be going. **You** have it. **You** *know* when you're off the path. **You** know when things don't feel right. Many people have these thoughts that "*things are right*" or "*things are wrong.*" Some listen and some don't. Many more say, "*Yes. This is my path. And I'm going to walk it. And I'm going to follow it. And I'm going to help as many as I can along the way stay on their path.*"

And that's what Creation is all about at this time. That's what Creator is wanting us to choose. We need to make these choices. When things are very bleak for us and very hard, we make these **good, right choices** over and over and over again. We need **choices** because He knows you ***know*** Divine Law. He knows you ***know*** the *Divine Path.*

He knows you ***know*** your calling. He knows you are **listening** to that little, small voice that says, "*This is what you need. This is what you do. And I would do it.*"

Remember that song when you were in grade school? And if not grade school, then vacation Bible school? *"This little light of mine, I'm gonna let it shine, let it shine, let it shine. This little light of mine, I'm gonna let it shine . . . all over God's world."*

When we make a **good choice** it makes His heart *sing*. He is always ready and he is waiting and he is willing to be there for anyone who calls out to Him. When we are willing to travel on our path. Or even when we get off our path, say, *"Help. I need to get back on my path. What should I do?"* We have to call out to Him. That's the secret. We must ask. You have to always ask. That's what we must do. That's what all the workers for the Light must do.

Everyone has hard days, but there's always that Light. Everyone gets discouraged. Everyone wants to *blame* some days. And if you see that Light you can go as far as you *want* to go, you *choose* to go.

# The Light Warriors

The Light Warriors are working now. The ones of you that are working together so diligently, helping many along the way, are the ones who are *100 percent* involved in Creator's work. And, there are some who are two per cent involved in Creator's work. And that's okay, because that two per cent is growing. And it is getting lighter and brighter and shinier. And the involvement in Creator's work is building and building and building. Soon it will be ***100 percent!***

I see the **Army of Light Workers**. And they have ropes. And they have the ropes pulled tight over their shoulders. They are pulling up a hill. They are *dragging* a platform behind them, a sled of "*slackers*," shall we say. Pulling. Pulling them *into the* ***LIGHT!***

They are pulling up the slackers because they **know** in their heart-of-hearts, they **know** they are not going to leave even them behind. They know that if the slackers can just get a little **spark** of that Light from them, they will jump off that sled and *start pulling their own weight.* That I can see is what you have been doing. You've been pulling that sled. And every once in a while, some will jump off and pull the sled with you, will keep pulling that sled with you. They will jump off and jump off. And more and more—**know** that more and more—are jumping off that sled. And they are *running* and they are *pulling* and they are moving *faster* and *faster* up the hill toward . . . there's a big sign up there. It's the goal: "***You are going to go home.***" And you're going bring as many as you can with you into the **Light**, into the **Sunshine**, into the **LOVE**, into the **New Millennium**. Many of you have pulled that sled for so long, for so hard. You've got those heavy work boots on, those heavy work boots, and you're pulling that sled. **Know** that your work does not go unnoticed.

This image is so explanatory of what is happening at this particular time. You, many of you, you are pulling your weight and you are pulling many behind you. And they continue to jump off. And they continue to say, "*Oh, I'll help. I do not ride. I see what it is I need to do.*" You are gonna get there. You are right where you are supposed to be. And maybe you're a little bit ahead of schedule.

We can't slack off. We can't slow down. We've gotta keep the pace and momentum going! And, we're gettin' there! Creator is preparing a Magnificent Feast, a Great Feast for us when we do arrive.

Suddenly, like an old-time southern Mammy, Grandmother SilverStar sings a Gospel Song, *"An' we gonna walk around' Heaven all day."*

D brightens to the sound, "That's right. That's right. Yes! Yes! We like that. Mammy sings it all the time."

# The Indigo Children

The **Indigo Children** have been sent by Creator to help with **The Transition** into the **New Age**, the **New Time**. They are helping us move into the Light very rapidly. They are *fully charged! ready to go!* and *they are doing their own work!* They have a *knowing* of what they have *come* to do. We don't have to worry about *their spark*. They are **all spark!**

The **Indigo Children** are *Incredible Beings of Light and Energy*! They are the *Star Children* who have just been waiting! to come in to help us transition into this **New Era**, into this **New Vibrational Level**, this **New Higher Frequency**. They *hold* that frequency.

When I first came over, when I first crossed over, it was the **Spirit Children** who taught me how to work with the energy. At first, it was difficult for me to acclimate. It was the Children who taught me *how to work with the energy*. That's why I was able to *come *through* so quickly, because the **Spirit Children** worked with me.

---

* [By "*come through*" Grandfather d refers to a Spirit Guide of the Light "*coming through from the other side*," speaking through, channeling through a "*reader*." D is a Master Teacher known as a "Speaker." Using the third dimensional human body of a "*reader*" d now speaks his messages from the other side and gives messages from other *Spirits of the Light* of other Dimensions. During his lifetime, d mastered the Way of Channeling and opened more than one hundred readers to channel. D was strict and pure, and to this day, unerringly follows one solid protocol: "*We work **only** with entities from the Light and for the benefit of all.*" After one crosses over, it ordinarily takes some time before being able to utilize the energies of a reader's third dimensional body, to adjust to the voice, to get the right vibrations, to be heard clearly. Amazingly, with the help of the Spirit Children, just days after crossing over, Grandfather d "*came through*" directly with his first message. Quite unusual! Quite a master!

In the last conversation SilverStar had with d, she asked, "*D, would you like to write a chapter for the Spiritual Awakenings book Grandmother Wolf is preparing?*" He paused, then turned and started walking down the path to his house, thinking. then turned back to her, "*We'll see . . . You know me. I can't write it. I can speak it.*" Prophetic! Two days later, D crossed over and within a week began channeling. The deeper meaning of d's words struck SilverStar so she approached Grandmother Wolf, "Now *I will ask d again to see if he wants to speak a chapter from the other side.*" D said, "*Yes *"and the readings were arranged with *The One Whom*

Grandfather d continues, "*The One Whom Many Children Love* works with Spirit Children who *know*, who *understand* the frequencies. There are *Angel Children* and then there are *Spirit Children*. They work together. They helped me understand my capabilities when I crossed over. They were the teachers. They were the ones that fine-tuned my abilities. It was the Children. We adults have forgotten how to work with energies. The light and the energy of the **Indigo Children** is so pure and so fine and so wonderful. They are "*hummingbird.*" Their energy is *hummingbird.*

They have brought in and carry a great deal of knowledge. They all have their own special gift to present to mankind. (It will be disclosed at a later time. Not at this moment.) Their skills are so finely tuned that it's almost hard to describe their capabilities. Creator is very pleased with His GIFT to Mankind—**The Indigo Children**—onto all the continents, all of the different aspects of humanity, all cultures, all countries, all worlds, and all universes. He loves us that much that he gave us the **Indigo Children**. He

---

*Many Children Love.* Just as d had said, "*I can speak it.*" SilverStar laughed, "*Yes! d, you did an Old Indian 'sneak-up' on me!*" As the work began, Spirit Guide *Katherine of the Light* explained, "*Before you three incarnate, you made a Sacred Contract to do this work.*" Using "The Way of the Channeling," Shaman d (Ancestor of the Light), Grandmother SilverStar (Native American Elder), and *The One Whom Many Children Love* (Native American Elder) had agreed to continue the readings for Creator. They did not suspect that the reader would be d, channeling from the other side, with SilverStar and *The One Whom Many Children Love* carefully following the teachings he had meticulously given them through the years. In a few short moons, this team—*seen and unseen*—completed what was to be the first of five chapters.

wants it to be smooth for us to transition into the New Time, into the New Place, into the New Beginning.

SilverStar responds, "May I ask you a question? Is the word *"Indigo Children"* interchangeable with *"Star Children"*?

D explains, "There are many of us who are *Star Children*—older *Star Children*. But these *New Star Children* that have been coming into our lives in the last six, seven years have Special Gifts. They are that special group called *"Indigo Children."* They are a Special Gift from God to Mankind. They are Wondrous Beings. They can do many things that it took me my entire life to learn. Yet they come in with this knowledge—this *Star Knowledge*—understanding of the World, understanding of Creator, understanding of the Universes. And it is just a *Knowing*. No one has to explain to them how to Meditate. No one has to explain to them how to Manifest. No one needs to explain to them how to Heal, how to Sing, how to Accomplish Wondrous Things. It is there. It is theirs!

So, there are *"Star Children"* and there are *"Indigo Star Children."* All **Indigo Children** are **Star Children**. But not all **Star Children** are **Indigo Star Children**. So, in some ways *"yes"* it is interchangeable. And, there is a distinction. And there is also a distinction in their gifts and their vibration and their color.

As an example, *The On whom Many Children Love's* grandchild \*\*H. has the Gift of Feeling Energies and of experiencing what energy was being sent with an item. That is

---

\*\* [*The One Whom Many Children Love* has a two-year old granddaughter who lives in another state. Without being told who a gift is from, this Indigo Child feels and identifies her Grandma's energy on a book or toy sent in the mail. Aware that her Indigo

this Indigo Child's GIFT—of Knowing Energies. Many have this GIFT. And there are other GIFTS also that are wonderful: There is the GIFT of being able to recognize certain energies whether it is love, happiness, joy, sadness, sorrow, anger, pain.

There is a boy that *The One Whom Many Children Love* works with in her practice who is a Star Child. He is an Indigo Child, and he is a very Old Soul who has come back in with GIFTS. His GIFT is his ability to clear and clean certain parts of Nature, of Mother Earth. He is developing his knowing of how much is too much to transmute and how much is optimal. At times when he has an appointment with *The One*

*Whom Many Children Love,* he is grateful that she can clear him off and send the excess away. So when he comes in, he knows what he gets to do. He knows that when he leaves her office he's going to be shining and clean and ready to go to work again. And each time it gets easier and easier for him to do his work, to do his cleaning and do his clearing. And *he* keeps it between, in boundaries, so to speak. So no one has to teach him how to do the clearing. That is a *given*. But controlling it is the process. He's getting used to using his gift in this dimension.

This ability to cleanse is a very, very important quality that many **Indigo Children** carry. It is a different kind of cleansing than what you (SilverStar) do, than what *The One Whom Many Children Love* does. It is *a vibrational way* much like the **Christ Light** (Reiki) . . . without special training. It's not been needed to be passed on to them. They are *born with it*. Yes. It is there *within them* to work with others, to love them, to clear them. It is their *choice*. Creator has made sure they come in *knowing their*

Grandchild will pick up her energy, before *The One Whom Many Children Love* sends a gift, she infuses it with love.]

*choices.* It's no mistake that certain Children are being placed in very strategic, very important places in society, in the world. **THEY KNOW WHAT THEIR JOB IS!** And they are taking care of it.

Up until the incarnation of the **Indigo Children**, mankind, when they incarnated (as with N., as with *The One Whom Many Children Love*, as with you) it took a while for their gifts to come through. For example, had \*\*\*N. been an Indigo Child and met M. at the time he did, the two could have been together forever because *all of his gifts would have come through.* And he would have recognized poor choices at a very early age.

When these new **Indigo Star Children** incarnate, they are *ready to go.* The **Indigo Children** come through with that *understanding of right choices* and that *spark.* They plunge in to Creator's work. They say, *"I'm here and ready to go!"* And, *"Let's see what Creator wants us to accomplish today! All righty, Folks!"*

And, for some of you, it has taken . . . it is a very long process. This has been the difference in the Star Children before and the Star Children now who are the **Indigo Children. Indigo Children** come out with their shields on and their swords up!

------

\*\*\*  [Here Grandfather d suggests the sharing of the story of N. and M., two Star Children who met and married when M., the elder Star Child, was 44 years old and N., the younger one was 22. After some years, the marriage ended. Grandfather d knew them both and is referring to the rough times they had because the younger of the two Star Children's gifts were not awakened, were not yet *coming through* as would have been true of an Indigo Star Child who would have been able to recognize poor choices. Thus, as Grandfather said, *"The two could have been together forever."*]

They are ready to go! *"All right, folks, I am here! and I'm ready to go. Let the games begin!'*

Grandmother SilverStar: *What you are saying makes me think of *Little Star.*

(d and SilverStar are referring to a five-year old **Indigo Star Child** whose given name actually is "*Star.*")

D responds, "Yes. And Little *Star* Child is learning about her powers. Remember the day she was visiting a friend and she hit the friend's dog very inappropriately? Star Child, Star Indigo Child, had become aggressive. It was most confusing to everyone who knew her. And, it was a giveaway from the dog. Star felt very bad about hitting the puppy. She INSTANTLY knew what she had done. Many children her age never . . . it takes them years to figure it out. It took her one time. One time. She understood. That was within her. She understood. It will never happen again. She understood. She understood m*ean*. She understands vicious. She understands kindness and gentle. She got it. And that was a Good giveaway that the dog presented to her. So, it was okay. If she would have continued to do that kind of abuse, the mother would have put on, "*This is not good. You cannot do this. This is not acceptable behavior.*" But she got it. She immediately got it.

*"One Time Learning."* **Indigo Star Children** have it.

There are different levels of coming in, incarnating. You start in kindergarten. You go through the twelfth grade. You go to college. You've got four years. And if you go to graduate school you've got two, four years of any kind of special training.

These kids come in at wherever their gifts are. Just ready! We're talking 12th grade! They come in in the 12th grade. And they are ready to go with their gifts. They know what their purpose is. They come in knowing what Creator wants and needs them to do. And they do it without any searching, as you searched, as I searched, just as many of us have searched. The **Indigo Children**, they don't have to search. The two of you are on the Master level. You are in post-graduate. These kids come in and they are already in college.

So, you can see there's, there's this HUGE help—the **Indigo Star Children**—that Creator has given us to push that sled up, to push up those slackers that are on that sled, just pushing them, they are just being pushed right up that hill. And then those on the sled, they'll have to look at themselves and say, "*Aw-oh*" and *know* that they slacked. They recognize that they are not pulling their own weight, that they are not making steps, that they are not doing what they need to do, and that they are not making good choices. As they begin to see more Light come into themselves, they will begin to understand. They will understand that this is, this is "*advancement*"—"*my advancement.*" I'm holding everybody back.

# *Spiritual Awakening*

My ***spiritual awakening*** came over a period of 60 years. It was a very slow, slow process. It was a very difficult process. It took a great deal of concentration, of focus of purpose, of having total control of my mind . . . where no one could interfere on my path.

My *spiritual awakening* was not on a timetable. There was no *"on such and such a date I will be awakened."* No, it was not like that. It was a very slow, slow process. It was day to day. It was meditation. It was the years and years of reading and studying and doing readings with other individuals.

My light work started with *this one helping to take children to the Light.

---

\* [By "*this one*" Grandfather d is referring to *The One Whom Many Children Love*, the Reader through whom he is channeling. Many years ago, in their sessions together, Grandfather d and *The One Whom Many Children Love* began to help 'lost children' on the other side return *Home to the Light*. Many Children who have been abused during a lifetime on Earth do not know about Love. No one has ever loved them so how would they know about Creator's Love? When they die, they wander this world looking for someone to help them. So, Grandfather d and *The One Whom Many Children Love* began their spiritual work together helping "lost children go home."

Respectfully Grandfather d explains, "When we refer to this one "*The One Whom Many Children Love*" and "the children," the majority, the greater percentage of those children, are the ones that she has "taken home." They are not the ones that she has known in this life. There have been many children she has known who love her. But "*The Children*" refers to children she has taken home." When we say "*The One Whom Many Children Love*" it refers to the one who has taken home to Creator so many 'lost children'. "It is her Father *Wa sha nu* who is the one who originally gave her that name. In the Indian way "*The One Whom Many Children Love*" is "*E cha* ta." It is very beautiful. It is the ancient pronunciation for *The One Whom Many Children Love*. There was a prophecy. It was foretold many eons ago that there would be

As I walked my path, as I did my Light work, Creator was not standing with his hands on his hips saying, *"You have to do this. I want you finished in so much time."* He just smiled. And He was happy to see me taking those steps. Whether they were baby steps, whether they were giant steps, it did not matter to Him, only that I was taking those steps and that I was doing exactly what HE knew, He knew in my heart I wanted to do. It wasn't because someone said, *"YOU do this! And YOU do this NOW!"*

_____

*"one to come to take the Children home."* Even though much of this has been lost, there is an Old One, a Grandmother, there is one Old One who knows of this prophecy. Give this Grandmother that name, *The One Whom Many Children Love, E cha ta.* She will know the background. She can give you all the information of this prophecy. She recognized *The One Whom Many Children Love* the first time she saw her. Grandmother held the Silence until the appropriate time would come. Yes, it was a prophecy that was foretold. Grandmother will recognize the name."

Grandmother SilverStar adds, "Hearing that this old prophecy has come true, that *The One Whom Many Children Love* has come, will help lift the people's spirit. To hear of a Good Prophecy Coming True will be a Great Gift for the People's Hearts. We are struggling here. We're wobbling, you know. Good Words strengthen. Strengthen our spirit. People understand that *Thread That Goes Through.* Our spirit understands *Things That Are As They Were Told To Be.* Our spirits understand that *Good Things are Coming in a Divine Way.*"

Grandfather d states, *"Truth is Truth. And when Truth is read, they know. It is as when you share something with each other you know:* **This is the Truth. There is a knowing that comes through.**"]

It was because *"I"* wanted to do this. And *"I"* wanted to do it for Creator. That's what spiritual awakening was about for me.

And when we get upset and when we get concerned about what we do, all we have to do is look at it and say, *"Is this what Creator wants me to do?"* And if the answer is *"yes,"* Then, *"Am I doing everything humanly possible to do what I am supposed to do for Creator?"* And if the answer is *"yes,"* then you have no worries. YOU HAVE NO WORRIES.

Each of us has our own spiritual talents, our own spiritual direction. No one can show you the right way to go. You have to put yourself in that *inner place*. That's what spirituality is: Connection to Creator. Connection! How strong that connection is. How strong that **LOVE** is. How strong that inner message is. The message is from Creator. Of course, you have to listen to it. As long as you know in your Heart that you are listening to His voice and no one else's, it's a very easy path. It's the very way to handle life on this Earth. Just take it a step at a time. So, say, "What am I doing? Am I going the right direction?" And, if in your Heart you know you are right, then you are making the right choice.

Grandfather addresses SilverStar, "This spiritual work you are doing you committed to hundreds of lifetimes ago. It's not about just this week, about this month. This has taken billions of lifetimes of planning. It isn't something that one fine day you wake up and you say, *"This is what I'm going to do. I'm going to write a Star Book."* No.

When you begin to question yourself, when you begin to wonder about your choices and whether you are doing the right thing, then you say, *"Creator, what do you want me to do?"* *"Is this what you want?"* And if your Heart says *"yes,"* then you know. If your Heart doesn't speak, then you also know.

When you are *spiritual,* you can hear your Heart. You can also hear other people's Hearts, other people's Minds. It is your Heart that is the Language of Love. It is the Language of Creation. It is Communion with the Holy Spirit. It is not through a telephone. It is not over the air waves. The real spirituality comes through the Heart, comes to the Heart. It is always through the Heart. If you argue over it, it's not spirituality. It ain't about what everyone else thinks and does. When your Heart speaks, you know. It doesn't come from anyone else. You know who put it there in the very perfect place of that Heart. You know it's the right thing to do.

You know, no matter how difficult it is, you have to walk through. You can do it. You can walk through this. We know it looks very bleak right now. There have been others who have felt and known exactly what you have experienced. That, *"getting through this"* is what the core is, is what is the process, knowing—beyond a shadow of a doubt—that you are on the right path that you are following your Heart's desire. Often people wonder if it's going to be okay. Following your Heart is the thing to do. You can follow your Heart.

The **Indigo Children**, they were born listening to their Hearts. They come into this world knowing what it took me eighty nine years to learn: Listen to your Heart. They come into this world knowing who they are, where they are going, and what their Heart tells them. That far surpasses anyone else.

It took me eighty nine years to get to that point of listening to my Heart, of following my Heart. The **Indigo Star Children** know they are eighty nine years ahead of everyone else who *"think"* they are connected, who *"think"* they are *"completely spiritual."*

It's there.

It's there for you anytime you have questions.

Listen to your Heart.

Connect to Great Spirit and know it's going to be taken care of.

We are in that time and place that

IT WILL BE DONE.

# CHAPTER TWO

## Our Relationship with Our Fellow Man

In the first chapter, we have talked about *"Our Relationship with Creator."* Now, we are going to talk about how *our relationship with each other is a service to Creator*. In one of his teachings Mohammad said, *"If you care about Allah, then go out and take care of your fellow man."* This teaching runs through many of the important religions of the world:

> *If you love Creator,*
>
> *if you love the Supreme Being,*
>
> *if you love Allah,*
>
> *if you love God,*
>
> *then care for your fellow man.*
>
> *Take care of those who are weak and are unable to care for themselves.*
>
> *Take care of the old.*
>
> *Take care of the young.*
>
> *Take care of the injured who are unable to care for themselves.*

***There is no greater love than to focus on caring and giving for Children.***

The *tsunami* was one way that mankind has recognized the *importance of the children of the world*. Of all of the individuals who died, a great portion were very young children or very old people. They were the adults who could not get away and the children were too young to know what to do. So, after this great loss of life, now there is a heightened awareness of *"we have to take care of those who are vulnerable."*

In the Indian Way, the Tribal Way, the Aborigine Way, we have always *valued the Children*; we have always *valued the very old*. Throughout time, the Children and the Elders have been our treasures. They are not put away somewhere to not have to be seen. They are cared for. They are in the home. They are part of the Family. The Elders are an important piece of The Extended Family. The Elders are the ones who are The Teachers. The Elders are The Ones Who Carry Inner Knowledge. The Elders share The Knowledge with the Children. The Elders are The Ones Who Teach the Children.

*Our relationship with our fellow man* is not just about our family, but is about the Family of Mankind. There is no greater gift than the Gift of Family. A Tribesperson was to *take of his family, to take care of his children, to take care of the elderly in the family*. In the Indian Way, in the Tribal Way, there is no greater honoring than those two aspects of the culture. There is no greater honor than to show one's love and respect through service to the Children and to the Elderly. "Walk the Talk," is the Indian Way. "Put your love for your Children and your Elders into acts of love. To a certain extent, there are many segments of society that have forgotten this very important honoring.

*Honoring the Children and Honoring the Elders needs to be brought back to all aspects of society.*

Right now, there are many Indigo Children on Mother Earth who are working very hard to help Mankind. Children who are not Indigo Children are very valuable, but the Indigo Children are even more so because *they hold the keys to our future.* They know where Creator wants us to go. They know how to get there. They know how to get there in the most expedient way, without delay, without interference. They know the things to do to *move through.* They know how to do the loopholes, how to do the zigzags. They're born with that understanding; it is an *intuition* in them.

Children of today have many more Helpers. They come into this life with more Guides, more Angels, more Helpers than Children did one hundred, two hundred years ago. It used to be that there was one Angel, one Helper, and one Spirit Guide. Now there could be as many as five, six, and seven depending on the task of the individual child.

And the Children are out there looking to see what they can to for their Fellow Man, are looking for how to help in this Time of Great Change and Great Celebration.

Each child has their own special areas, their own special gifts. And they are advanced in what they do. And they do it *intuitively.* They focus on Mankind, helping Mankind, being there to do what they need to do to make things go smoothly. The Children are in service to all. And the Children understand *love of service.*

There's a song "*the wind beneath my feet.*" The Indigo Children are "*the wind beneath Mankind's feet.*" The Children are going to *propel* Mankind into this New Age, this New Time, and this New Reality.

One of the verses of the Bible teaches, "*Do unto others as you would have them do unto you.*" "*Love your fellow man. Love your neighbor.*"

In the future certain thought forms will be gone from the Minds of the People of Earth. Future thought is not going to be about loving someone because they are White, because they are Baptist, because they are whatever socio-economic characteristics that identifies that group. Humankind is stripping that away. We will realize that these things do not matter.

It does not matter how much money the person makes.

It does not matter what he does.

It does not matter who his parents were or whether they were in prison

or whether they were abused or mistreated.

It only matters that when you are with your fellow man,

you love that individual, and

you give to that individual, and

you show him that unconditional love is within their reach.

If one person goes out and touches five people,

> and they go out

> and each of those people touch five people,

> it won't be long before every one will be touching everyone else—

> on *all* continents,

> in *all* places of the world.

There will be no more bitterness or hatred or deceit.

Life will be about something bigger and stronger and more beautiful.

# How You Treat Others in Business

How you treat others in business impacts the world, impacts civilization. For too long the focus has been about survival of the fittest. In past thought, there has been an overriding desire to focus on, *"Am I going to make money at this? Am I going to make money at that?* "That thinking is going to be a thing of the past. Mankind's work is not about that anymore. It's not going to be about if you have this and this and this and this thing and what is important to you is the bottom line, how much money you're gonna make, achieve, how much money is there for you to have. It's not gonna be *"I'm gonna do this and this and this because I'm gonna make a lot of money."* It will be obsolete to think in those terms. It will be a thing of the past. No one will be thinking, *"Well, how much am I gonna make?" "Am I gonnna make this?"* or *"Am I gonna make?' "Am I gonna get paid for that?"* No one.

Our work for Creator is not about the money. Such thought will be a thing of the past. A Human Being will do something because she loves to do it, not because *"I'm gonna get this amount of money for it."* You will work because you love the job you do. You love what you can accomplish. You love the changes you see in the lives of others because of what you do.

You are going to be paid what *you are worth!* And that's going to be an easy thing because everyone is going know what their worth is. Our hearts will be open. Each person's value will be clear.

The work you (*No tlv si A d elv U ne ga,* SilverStar) and This One (*E cha ta,* The One Whom Many Children Love) do, could you put a price tag on it? Could you say, *"Okay this work is worth this much."* No, there is no one who could do that.

Also, let me assure you that the worry of existing and getting by is going to be a thing of the past, particularly for you two, because you cannot put a dollar value on the kinds of services and gifts you give to others. It is simply a given: You are going to be recognized for the healers you are. It's not going to be about, *"Am I going to make it here? Am I going to make it there. Is this going to be enough to cover that?"* Material existence is not going to be something you are going to have to worry about anymore.

I know we've said this before, and hard times have kind of lingered on from time to time. But that's been one of the big changes that's been going on with the two of you *this last week. You are going to another level. You are moving to another level.

We are going to have an early spring **this year. Mother Earth will be warm soon, making it easy to plant and get out there and have your garden and have good food to eat. And you are not going to have to worry about what you are going to have to eat because you're gonna have fresh fruits and vegetables. And it's gonna be warm here not cold as in the past. There is a global warming taking place. It's time. [These Earth changes are things the government people are talking about in their own circles, but they are leary about putting out there to the people.] Everyone has been aware of Mother Earth's changes. A part of us is afraid of change.

---

\* (The first days of February 2005.)
\*\* (The Spring of 2005.)

# Love, Joy and Happiness

Fear is will be a thing of the past. The thought form of fear will be completely *removed* from human memory. If there is no fear, then there is only **love**. If there is only **love** and there is only **joy** and there is only **happiness**, you don't want to fight. You are **joyful** and **happy** and **loving**.

This is how Creator wants us **all** to be. He wants us to be **joyful**. He wants us to be **happy**. He wants us to be content with our lives, with our careers, with our families, with the significant others in our life. He *wants* us to be **happy**.

And, if He wants us to happy, if He wants us to be successful, if He wants us to be content, then He's going to send us the things that we need so that we can be all of those things. And He's going to take away the things that we don't need.

This is the best of times. We are living in a time when it couldn't be any more beautiful than it is right now. **This is a time of great love, great joy, great happiness.**

SilverStar says, "*Ga li e li ga*. I am grateful. We've been climbing' uphill to get here."

Well, yes, you have. And there are few others who have worked as hard as you two have worked to get to that place of love, of joy, of happiness.

Different realms have needed to be cleaned up. Different parts of the country have needed to be purified. Different parts of the *world* have needed to be cleared up, cleaned up so that

Mother Earth can move up to another level. So this other work, this purification had to be completed—completely finished—before this new piece of **love** and **joy** and **happiness** could go in place. The Light Workers had to complete the work of taking the lost souls home, taking the lost children home, clearing up Mother Earth, and the great work of taking all of the negativity off of this planet. Washing it away. Washing it clean.

The Light Workers have worked incredibly hard for us to get to this place, this level of **Purity**, of this frequency of **Light**, this frequency of **Love**. And, as I said previously, more and more are making **good choices**, are picking up their **sacred responsibility**, and are moving on with what they need to do to help their Fellow Man. **Human Beings are moving forward at a rapid pace**.

SilverStar responds, *"This is really good news."*

# CHAPTER THREE

## Commitments

There are *commitments* that we humans come in to life on Earth with, *specific kinds of *commitments*. To make our plan, our commitments for an incarnation, we meet with the Spiritual Hierarchy and with the individual guides who will be following us through the incarnation. We decide *with* the Spiritual Hierarchy and everything is cleared *through* the Hierarchy. Together we look at life questions such as: *What do you need to work on? Where do you want to go with this? What kind of experiences do you need? What do you need to get to this end goal?* Then, we make those commitments. We make them to Creator.

Moving up or down on the ascension ladder depends on the choices an individual makes in each lifetime. Each of you has had *specific long-range goals.* For this one, *Echata*, The One Whom Many Children Love, the goal of lifetimes has been "taking the lost children home"—something that took her many, many thousands of years to accomplish. For you, SilverStar, the goal was completing the Star Knowledge Bundle. For thousands and thousands and thousands of years you have come back to accomplish this goal. You two are unique; your goals are much different than most. Furthermore, you have *earned* this time of attainment of your goal. You have worked hard to accomplish the goals of each lifetime. You have kept on track. If anything,

---

* The book *Sacred Contracts* does an excellent job of describing specific commitments in greater detail. *Sacred Contracts, Awakening your Divine Potential.* Copyright 2001. Harmony Books. New York, New York.

you have gone far and above what you needed to do to stay on your path.

So, one is one a long-range path. Many people need to come back thousands of times to grasp the *smallest* of the Principles of Creation: *To love your fellow man. To do unto others as you would have them do unto you.* Learning Creator's Principles is tedious, is a tough challenge. There are always many obstacles in the pathway, in everyone's pathway. There are challenges, tests that come up. Whether or not you surpass these challenges is really up to you. And, I have said before, some people whom I thought (when I was on Earth) were a shoe-in, that I perceived as *on track* . . . well, when I got to the other side and I saw what is really in their hearts. It was a rude awakening for me, and I thought to myself, *"Oh, my goodness."*

Creator knows what is in your *heart.* Creator *always* knows what's in your *heart.* He knows what's in *everyone's heart.* It is as we said, he knows from minute to minute, second to second, mini-second to mini-second. He knows from each point in time where everyone is on their path. Again, we can compare His knowing to a mother who knows where her child is on their growth path. So does Creator know where all of you are.

Here is an example of how this *knowing* occurs: Yesterday when this one, *Echata,* The One Whom Many Children Love, saw Miss Kitty there was an *energy pattern* that transferred from Miss Kitty to this one. There was a *knowing* that Kitty was not happy and that she was ready to leave. And this one sensed Kitty's feeling and was accurate. That was an example of *"picking up an energy."* This is how Creator knows. There is an energy *signature* that Creator picks up on, that He *reads.* On a subconscious *heart* level. Creator reads *heart messages.* And animals are *all heart.*

When they're angry or scared they might go into another level, but for animals around people, they're *all heart*.

So, as each individual comes into an earthly life, they have their **commitments** and they have **goals**. On one level, each one knows exactly what he has to do to accomplish these goals. So, before they come in, they are also aware of the **challenges** they will meet. And they will not know until after they pass on whether they've met those challenges, whether they've failed miserably or whether they've *far surpassed* whatever has been thrown in their way.

And it is then, when they cross over, that they find out. It is not Creator that is the one who judges us, it is ourself. When we look at our life choices, He is there with us to support us, guide us, to help us. But *we* are the ones that looks at *our choices* and the *effect that we have had on others*. He is there for us when we have to face those lows, those highs, those mediocre areas of choice. He is there with us to support us, to love us, to guide us, along with the Hierarchy, along with the White Brotherhood, along with the Angels of *AN, the Sisterhood of the Shields. There are many Archangels and Guardians out there helping us and leading us—as long as we stay in our *heart*. Now when we lose that heart focus, then we lose our perspective, then we lose what is nearest and dearest to us.

Kirlian photography is a way, an earthly method of looking at the *heart energy*. Kirlian photography of the human heart shows when someone has the ***Buddha's Heart***. When a person is in their heart, when their heart is open, this photography shows the difference. There is a change in the *light* around the

---

* AN is pronounced "on."

109

*heart* area. In many pictures of Jesus, of Mary, it is the *heart* area that *shines* out. It *glows*.

**The heart is the connection to Creator. It is the heart that is so strong. The heart is what leads us. The heart is what keeps us on our path.**

The *heart* must be *developed*. When we come in, *we are born with the heart connection to Creator*. Sometimes along the way some lose the heart connection; when the obstacles come in our way, it begins to fade. If we don't have the *heart connection* or we don't *go back* to that *heart connection,* then we can go off on the wrong road, on the wrong path and lose ground and lose the direction we need to be going.

When we incarnate, there is the plan that is set up and there are also safeguards and back-up plans. If we make choice "A," choice "B," choice "C," then we are going well. Now, if we make the wrong turn back there, there is also another plan, there is also an alternate, an alternate entity that might come in and maybe help us along or maybe intervene, get us back on our track, help us through a bad situation so we can make better choices. It is arranged, it is planned before we ever come into this life.

The movie *"The Five People We Meet in Heaven"* shows an example of an individual taking a look at his choices after crossing over: In this story, a man crossed over to Heaven. He thought he had been a failure. Actually, he had done incredible feats, wonderful things, and he had stayed right on his path. In fact, he had even gotten higher on his path than what he'd planned when he first incarnated. As his story progressed, the viewer could see the spiritual evolution of how A went to B and B went to C and C went to D and D went to E.

This movie gave this understanding in a nutshell, gave an overview of what happens when an individual makes *good choices*. You can see the choices this man made as the result of events in his life and relationships in his life, and how they were all key, key points in his life. Had one event not happened, then something else would have happened making it so that he was able to accomplish his major goal in this lifetime.

All of life's pieces are merging together to come out to give you the best experience, the best opportunity to grow and to succeed on this planet Earth.

Quite incredible!

# CHAPTER FOUR

## Accelerating Our Growth

We can accelerate our *growth*, our *light bodies*, and our *opportunities to serve Creator*

For example, you are going along and things are going really well and things are smooth, and you're accomplishing these things that you've worked very hard on in many eons of lifetimes.

For example, you SilverStar are carrying the Star Bundle. Then, Creator had something else He needed you to do. Therefore, He needed someone else to carry that bundle around. He put that word out in the ethers that 'we need someone else to pick up this Star Bundle for a few weeks so we can send this light worker out and do this particular job that needs to be taken care of'.

There are a select few light workers that accomplish this task. The request for help goes out to this group. And, because they are on a certain level, that is the group that it goes out to first.

This is not discrimination. You must be at a certain point before you are given a task. When you have finished the one task you chose to accomplish, then you are given a higher task.

This gives new meaning to "*God doesn't give you more than you can handle.*" In fact **you** are *requesting* more. Not only is He not giving you more than you can handle, *you are asking for more.*

When Creator asks for volunteers, "*Would you like to do this? Is this something you could help out with?* there will be a few hands go up. There may not be any hands that will go up. But it's rare, rare time that someone doesn't respond to Creator—a very very very small chance, small percentage.

There are many earthly and heavenly Light Workers. In the ranks of the angels, angels have certain tasks. There are angels that are a friend to the children. There are angels that are warriors that go into battle. They do whatever they need to do to protect mankind, to protect, specifically, the children. There are angels who are teachers. There are groups of angels who sing, who compose music all day. The same as there are different angels there are different humans who are on different levels. And this is true throughout *all* of the Universes, not just our Universe, *throughout all of the Universes.*

The new task that you did these last couple of weeks, SilverStar, was an important task. But had not someone come along to pick up the bundle you are carrying, then you could not have moved on to go do what you had volunteered for.

So, we are working hand in hand. Everyone is working together. We are connected. That was the basis and the beautiful part of "*Five People You Will Meet in Heaven.*" **We are all connected. We are all connected!**

One person does not go unnoticed. One person's chosen job is not more important than another person's chosen goal or responsibility. It is true we evolve as we keep coming back. The ones who keep doing what they need to be doing, keep that engine moving, moving' just as hard and as fast and as diligently as they can, their goals can be speeded up. They can accomplish, can fulfill their commitments quicker.

The Star Bundle was finished ahead of time, maybe ten years ahead of time. The Children were taken home thirty years ahead of time. You can't compare one to the other. They are both key pieces of evolution.

We are moving into a New Realm, into the ***Time of Peace and Love and Light***.

John Paul made a tremendous Giveaway when he crossed over. His choice to cross over came at a most opportune time. He knew *exactly* what Creator needed him to do. Creator needed people all over the world to open up their *hearts* and their *souls* and their *love* for each other. So, in service to all, John Paul crossed over and his funeral on the day of a solar eclipse opened the *hearts* of billions of human beings all at once. And the love in the open hearts of humanity wanted to be poured out so that ***we could move the last bit of negativity out of this world once and for all***.

All of these pieces have connected together. The human commitments and goals have come together for fine synchronicity. Manifesting pieces together is necessary. We are at a time now when, as long as a desire comes from the heart we can manifest whatever we chose. Desires from greed or the side that is selfish or mean will not manifest. Only desire from our *heart*, our heart's deepest desire, the desire coming from the Buddhist Heart can be manifested.

Some people say, "*Oh, that doesn't work. I don't believe in that.*" They are not coming from their *heart* and cannot manifest when they are not in their *heart.*

How well the *heart* is developed can be measured by the Kirlian photography. And as long as those individuals who have that greatly enhanced *heart* connection, that *heart connection* is to Creator. And as long as they follow that *heart,* as long as they look inside and they *know* that that *heart* feels **right** and **good**, then they *know* they've made the *right* choice.

And they can take a giant leap forward, can manifest whatever they need to for the betterment of all. Manifesting is not for selfish needs or wants. People who are self-centered and selfish and mean and unkind to others don't have that *heart connection.*

There will come a time when you talk to someone, you will know immediately know whether they are coming from their *heart* or whether they are coming from a much lower vibration. And it's going to be more and more difficult for people with a low vibration to survive on Earth. This is becoming a Star Planet. It is no longer a planet for the dark side. It is a **Planet of Light** and **Love** and **Peace** and **Joy**.

Superman PJs

Another Halloween

Pow N' Wow

Big House Doors And Pots To Climb

Rex

My Niece And Her Cows

She Loved To Kiss Me

niece and purple shirt

CJ not happy

Kiki And Joey          Mom can read, can't see.          The Suit

The Swing Set                              CJ

Joey Loved Hugs

Fisher Price Skater    Mom at my skating birthday party    My Favorite Christmas Picture

Echata      Joey's Girlfriend